Uprooted

Uprooted

Recovering the Legacy
of the Places We've Left Behind

GRACE OLMSTEAD

SENTINEL

SENTINEL
An imprint of Penguin Random House LLC
penguinrandomhouse.com

Most Sentinel books are available at a discount when purchased in quantity for sales promotions or corporate use. Special editions, which include personalized covers, excerpts, and corporate imprints, can be created when purchased in large quantities. For more information, please call (212) 572-2232 or email specialmarkets@penguinrandomhouse.com. Your local bookstore can also assist with discounted bulk purchases using the Penguin Random House corporate Business-to-Business program. For assistance in locating a participating retailer, email B2B@penguinrandomhouse.com.

Library of Congress Cataloging-in-Publication Data
Names: Olmstead, Grace, author.
Title: Uprooted : recovering the legacy of the places we've left behind / Grace Olmstead.
Description: New York : Sentinel, [2021] | Includes bibliographical references and index.
Identifiers: LCCN 2020038360 (print) | LCCN 2020038361 (ebook) |
ISBN 9780593084021 (hardcover) | ISBN 9780593084038 (ebook)
Subjects: LCSH: Communities—United States. | United States—Social conditions.
Classification: LCC HN57 .O6 2021 (print) | LCC HN57 (ebook) | DDC 306.0973—dc23
LC record available at https://lccn.loc.gov/2020038360
LC ebook record available at https://lccn.loc.gov/2020038361

Printed in Canada
1 3 5 7 9 10 8 6 4 2

Book design by Cassandra Garruzzo

For Grandpa Dad, Grandma Mom,
Grandpa Wally, and Grandma Elaine,
with love and gratitude.

Contents

Introduction

I step into a familiar graveyard. My husband is with me, and so is our oldest daughter, a curly-haired girl with dark lashes and thoughtful eyes. I am showing them the graves of my forebears, here where generations of my family rest in the soil of Emmett, Idaho.

I brush snow off gravestones, searching for names. There are my great-grandparents, known as Grandpa Dad and Grandma Mom, side by side in the earth. Nearby, I see the graves of Grandpa Dad's brothers, his sister, and his parents—along with dozens of other, more distant kin. My husband holds our daughter as he quietly reads inscriptions.

To visit these graves today, I had to travel twenty-four hundred miles: over the Blue Ridge Mountains and the Great Plains, past the Rockies and the Sawtooths. It is good to be home in this quiet land, where purple shadows line the foothills and the Payette River is shadowed by cottonwood trees. It is good to be here, in a place where the past is still present and preservation is paramount. But much has changed here since I was a child.

Fields that once were filled with corn and sugar beets, mint and onions are now graded, leveled, and covered with single-family homes. The farm stand where we bought tomatoes and peaches for canning is gone, empty—as are many of the small mom-and-pop businesses we frequented growing up. Everywhere I drive in my homeland, I see the past crumbling and fading away, increasingly paved over and forgotten. And even as I observe good changes, I mourn what's been lost and what we are losing.

I grew up surrounded by folks who committed themselves to this place for the long haul. They served and loved it, year after year. For many of them, including my great-grandparents, rootedness meant turning down bigger paychecks, adventure, excitement, and ease. But they were able to experience the wonder of each season, the pride of committed stewardship. They got to grow old next to the ones they loved—and got to watch a new generation of young folks, like me, grow up in the land they had tended.

Now boom-and-bust cycles and the exodus of the young, including me, have worn down the threads of community and belonging. Many of the valley's rooted individuals are still alive—but they are growing old.

I learned my first stories about this town at the feet of my Grandpa Dad, who was an aged farmer by that point. He knew all his neighbors, and they knew him. He was out riding his tractor until his early nineties, attending church services and teaching Sunday school until the end of his days. Over his lifetime, this valley aged into postindustrialism and decay. I am sure that much of what he saw alarmed him, inspiring in him a sense of sorrow for the land's lost past, its fading local culture. I think that is why he told me stories over and over again, making sure I would not forget the ones who came before us, the countryfolk that history books would ignore. To Grandpa Dad, their stories mattered. And so they mattered to me as well.

Not everyone believes small towns matter. In 2015, Kevin Williamson wrote for *National Review* that "some towns are better off dead."[1] The prevalent national attitude, at least among many conservatives and libertarians, seems to be that we need to let communities evolve according to the dictates of the market. Protesting change is not only fruitless, it is backward and illogical. "Get the hell out of Dodge, or Eastern Kentucky, or the Bronx," Williamson wrote. Leave the broken places behind. Rootedness, these writers seem to suggest, is an antiquated philosophy toward life: a nostalgic attitude that ought to be abandoned.

The suggestion that leaving is the answer rubbed me the wrong way—because the more I studied the history of my own community, the more I realized that most of its struggles with depletion and brokenness were caused by those who leave. The only time things were mended and restored were the times when someone, somewhere, chose to stay.

In my first few years living in Washington, DC, I wrote many articles defending broken places—fighting for people's decisions to stay in hurting places of the world, fighting for towns experiencing postindustrial collapse or brain drain.

But it felt hypocritical: How could I argue for these things when I had left Idaho behind? When I was living in one of the most prosperous areas of the United States, working in one of the most important and bustling cities in America?

Now, in the graveyard, I am haunted by these questions. What do I owe the past? What do I owe the people who invested in the land that raised me? What do I owe the places where I'm from? Should I return, for my own sake and for the sake of the communities that gave me life?

For several years now, I have felt as if my feet were planted in two different places, two very different sets of soil. I have experienced a deep sense of tension between the person I was and the person I've become, and have long wondered when or whether I should choose between these two identities, these two places.

It could be too late for me to move back. Virginia is now the place where I have worked and walked and worshipped for more than ten years. It's the place where I've attended town meetings, made new neighbors, and cultivated close friendships. Returning to Idaho would mean forsaking the roots I've started to send down in my new community.

But something has to change. The place I love is hurting. The ways of life that bound people together are disintegrating. The homogenization of farmland and isolation of farmers, proliferation of food deserts, decline of regional commerce and industry clusters, deterioration of soil and water, and suburbanization of farmland that plague this rural land will destroy not just individual lives but our food sources if we can't reclaim our roots.

Will I go back? I don't know. This book is my ode to the past, an attempt to pay back the debt I owe. It's an attempt to push back against the exploitation and extraction that have become part of our economy and our moral calculations. It's an homage to the "nobodies" who maintain our unknown places today.

But most of all, it's an exercise in discernment. Sooner or later, I will have to make a choice.

Uprooted

Chapter One

It is a cold, quiet November morning. The smoke from California's devastating wildfires has finally dissipated from the Idaho air, but now a dense fog has taken its place. I am visiting home for a while, back in the brick house where my parents have lived for more than twenty-five years. Now, as I drive from Fruitland toward Emmett, I see a flock of geese flying south. Cattle graze on either side of the road, their breath steaming. The butte rises sharply in the distance, covered in deep purple shadows. One Emmett resident once noted on Facebook that when light hits the north side of the butte just right, it looks like the velvet on a deer's antler: "silvery, surreal, and beautiful."

I pull into the parking lot for Emmett High School. It's the first monolithic dome school ever built, constructed in the 1980s for its affordability and unique look. It's also supposed to be pretty energy efficient. But I've heard that many of the students hate it; they are jealous of kids over the hill, in cities like Meridian, who are getting new, expensive high school buildings with walls of brightly lit windows. The city of Emmett has struggled to get bonds passed to make school improvements.

I walk to the school's agriculture building, a mini dome a short walk from the larger 180-foot-diameter school building. Inside, Nate Low—head of the agricultural science and technology department at the school—is talking to an advisory group of students who are interested in agriculture. The students look at me curiously as I walk through the door and sit down. I quickly tally them up in my head. There's more than thirty students in this class. After Mr. Low introduces me, I stand and walk to the front of the classroom.

"I grew up in Fruitland, down the road, but my grandpa and great-grandpa farmed here in the Emmett Valley," I tell them. "Now I'm a journalist, working outside Washington, DC, and I am writing a book about agriculture in this area. I would love to hear more about your hopes for the future and whether you're interested in farming long-term." I pause. "Would you be okay with my taking a quick poll?"

The students nod.

"Okay. How many of you are interested in being a farmer or rancher after you graduate?" I ask.

About three-quarters of the students raise their hands.

I make a note. "Awesome. Now how many of you want to stay in Emmett after you graduate?"

Three students slowly raise their hands. A few others giggle quietly.

I write down the number and circle it. "If you'd like to talk to me more about your interest in farming, I'll just be over here in the corner," I say with a smile.

A little later, five students—four girls and a boy—sit down across from me. They look excited and slightly nervous. One of them tells me she'd love to be a farmer's wife or to help run a dairy someday. Another, from the nearby tiny town of Sweet, says he wouldn't mind taking over his dad's operation after graduation. A couple of them tell me that leaving Emmett is something they all talk about—but something they doubt kids will follow through on. Everybody likes to sound too good for this place. But a lot of them love it underneath the surface.

I'm not so sure, though. I just talked to a Baptist pastor here in town. He told me there's a single young man in his congregation, probably about thirty years old, who is one of the last members of his graduating class still living in Emmett. Everybody else has left him behind.

Despite their bravado, the students I'm talking to may not plan to leave home. They don't seem to have any concrete plans for exodus, just a sense that it's good to say you have big plans. What remains to be seen is what they do when they experience the appeal of greener pastures, the siren call of other places—more "important" places—that will beckon to them, as they did to me, in times to come.

For now, I enjoy watching these students lean over tables and talk quietly to each other, laughing and grinning and listening to Mr. Low. I enjoy seeing their eagerness as they tell me about the horses or cattle they help raise, the work they've done with

Future Farmers of America (FFA) and the agricultural department here at the high school. I enjoy sitting here, watching a new crop of Emmett students enjoy their time in this soil. For as long as it lasts.

My Grandpa Wally is a pepper-haired man with an infectious belly laugh who waltzed with me as a baby. He would put on his overalls and boots and work while the sun slumbered—often waking at or before 4 a.m. during harvest season. His sweet corn, fresh beef, and brown-speckled eggs filled our stomachs year-round. Face brown and wrinkled from the sun, eyes glinting with humor, his bass voice made the floor tremble. When I was a young girl—shy and unsure of myself, buried in books—he asked me where I intended to go to college. I told him I wasn't sure.

"Go to college out East," he said. "It'll help you become your own person and figure out who you want to be." Then, he added with a grin and a wink, I could become famous and write a book about him someday.

It was unlikely that any of us would venture so far from home. My family had lived in Idaho for generations. Our relationships were close, bound as we were by history, tradition, and love. My siblings and I would shuck sweet corn grown by Grandpa Dad (my great-grandfather, Grandpa Wally's father), sitting at a picnic table in my grandparents' backyard. Our hands worked fast as we piled gleaming cobs in a box to carry into the house, where Grandma Elaine and my mother were cutting it off the cob, cooking it with sugar, salt, and butter, then freezing it. Grandpa Dad sat beside me, wearing a black-and-red gingham shirt, his snowy hair forming a thick white cloud around his head. Grandpa Wally sat next to him, strong hands palming the ears and shucking them with practiced care.

Grandpa Dad's deep, velvety voice rang out as he told stories about his wife, Iva, who passed away from cancer before I was born. She would write little love notes and tuck them in Grandpa Dad's lunch box almost every day. She wrote them on little slips of paper, no bigger than fortune cookie messages. They said things like, "I love you to the moon and back." Often, Grandpa Dad would write little responses on the back for her and return the notes when he carried his lunchbox back inside at the end of the workday.

Over the course of his lifetime, Grandpa Dad dug many of the ditches that still feed water to crops in north Emmett—all of them with a spade and his two hands. By his nineties, his spine was bent and crooked, shaped by those long years of digging. His six-foot-one frame stooped low, bringing his face near to mine when I was still quite young.

Grandpa Dad would keep telling us stories until after we finished the corn. Grandma Elaine would make us dinner: a giant lasagna bubbling with cheese, or shepherd's pie piled high with mashed potatoes. Then there would be pie and coffee—rich, dark, black coffee—and we'd gather in the living room to listen as Grandpa Dad talked about watching silent movies as a child, and courting his beloved Iva. He was the first storyteller and historian I knew. His ninety-year-old mind was still sharp and vivid, overflowing with knowledge and narrative. I remember the poetry he shared with us around the dinner table—long verses that he would memorize while out riding his tractor.

Growing up in a farm community connected me to the land. But perhaps more so, it connected me to a past that offered glimpses of (and hopes for) the future. Driving through the quiet farmland and observing its seasons brought to mind people, meals, and stories from years gone by and a sense of what might come around again in the future. Participating in farm tradition was like taking your place in the dance: joining arms with the company behind and before. Family, food, soil, and place were all bound together in the rhythm of the seasons, and to be fed was to remember.

I never appreciated that time when living it. There was a casual, comforting reliability in it. There was no reason to expect anything else. Grandma's candles and china, her careful place settings—they never changed. Neither, I thought, would we.

But as I grew older, I struggled to find my place in the quiet river valley. I was known as Rick's daughter or Wally's granddaughter. My last name held more meaning for most people than my first. My siblings and I often laughed about the way that affected our life on a day-to-day basis, considering the people who were strangers to us, yet regarded us with a fondness and responsibility borne out of community ties. But I often wondered what it would be like to be known only for myself: for people to have no previous knowledge of those ties, and to take me only for who I was.

I also craved novelty. Nothing big seemed to hang in the

6

balance in our small town. Nothing noteworthy. Grit and dependency are important—but they can also be monotonous. (That is, in fact, their point: they are consistent.) The journeys of my favorite protagonists were, in contrast, anything but mundane: Frodo Baggins left the Shire on a quest that ultimately resulted in the salvation of Middle-earth. Jo March left home for New York City, seeking adventure beyond the stasis of Concord. Lucy Pevensie opened a wardrobe door and became the queen of a hidden country. Each had a quest, a mission: a calling beyond the quotidian. Belle, my favorite Disney princess as a toddler, was also the girl from a small town who sang plaintively, "There must be more than this provincial life!"

I began to think about attending college on the East Coast. I was eager to write about far-off lands and research injustices in other places—eager to explore a new patch of earth. I could pursue new adventures, foster my own rhythms and patterns, seek out a quest worth embarking on.

After all, Idaho did not need me, and I did not feel as if I belonged to it. I saw myself apart from place: a consciousness sculpted by family and education, literature and music, perhaps, but not by place. And so, eventually, Grandpa Wally's prediction came true.

My dad flew with me to Virginia the week of freshman orientation. I knew he was worried that if I left Idaho, I would never come back. But he didn't once protest my plan to leave home. He filled my pockets with quarters for laundry and took me out for ice cream. We'd forgotten to pack any photos or decor for my room, so he bought a little black picture frame and doodled some stick figures for me: representing him, my mom, my siblings, and my cat.

The last day, Dad hugged me and told me he was proud of me. After he left, I cried myself to sleep, feeling lonelier than I ever had. But I also felt hopeful and excited. I had wanted to forge new lines for myself. Here was my chance to forge them.

Throughout college, I fell in love with Virginia. The sprawling hills, covered in lush greenery, reminded me of Beatrix Potter's pictures of the English countryside. In the spring, my friends and I drove to see Washington, DC's cherry blossoms, or went to the park and enjoyed the sweet, rich smell of warming earth and the vibrant pink of the azalea bushes. We stayed up all night studying books ancient and new, debating philosophy, or concocting pranks. These were the sorts of kindred spirits I had searched for my entire life. And there was a feeling of excitement in the air, knowing we were on the verge of someplace "important": a city filled with politicians and diplomats, aides and scholars. My friends dreamed of becoming lawyers, judges, State Department officials, or humanitarian activists.

College enabled me to grow the part of myself thirsty for knowledge—the nerdy child who daydreamed through math and science and carried around books instead of purses. But it also gave me, for the first time, the opportunity to reflect on what it meant to be an Idahoan. Sometimes you don't sense or understand your roots, how they make you what you are, until you've been uprooted. That's what moving to the East Coast did for me. All of a sudden, I felt absences: the smell of pine when hiking in the woods, the taste of Grandma Elaine's pie on Sunday

[handwritten margin note: This was more to West Coast did for me.]

evenings. Those absences showed me little bits and pieces of myself that were owed to Idaho's soil and culture. Often, they filled me with a soft sense of nostalgia: an ache for home and its beauty.

That said, the homesickness I felt for Idaho in those days was relatively minor, easily dismissed. The absences and their eccentricities made for fun table conversation. But nothing more. I was too busy building out this new hunger, this new identity that allowed me to delve into philosophy and history and literature.

During my junior year, I met a handsome and kind young man in the U.S. Air Force and fell in love. We got married after I graduated and settled in Alexandria, Virginia. My husband commuted daily to Andrews Air Force Base, and I started working in Washington, DC: first as a magazine intern, then as an editorial assistant.

Every day, I raced past the commuter train's closing doors onto smudged and dirty orange carpet, clasped a metal pole, and watched Virginia's green countryside slowly fade into blackness. The train was always full, so I wrapped one arm around a pole and hugged a book to my chest, reading snippets when there was room enough to open it. I often felt intimidated by the dour people wearing important-looking badges and fancy leather shoes. Somber faces peered at phones, absorbed in the enormity of important emails and tasks awaiting them at the end of their commute.

Washington was full of brilliant, incisive people, many of whom could feel austere and closed—at least when compared to the people and culture of my youth. The first time my sister rode the Metro with me into the city, she looked around and whispered in alarm, "Why is everyone so sad?"

I had made a new life for myself and joined in another Idaho tradition—albeit one that few other members of my family had participated in historically. I was now part of the so-called brain drain.

For as long as Idaho has been settled, people have come and gone as things got hard, as the land or community demanded more love of them than they were willing or able to give. Cycles of conquest and depletion, boom and bust, have gone on so long that they now seem normal. Few of us realize how much we have lost in the process—how much has blown away over those centuries of boom and bust and decay.

Indeed, even as I rode that train with quiet strangers, plunging past green countryside into dark tunnels, I was completely oblivious to my role in that decay and loss. Although I ached for what I had left behind, turning the memories over and over in my mind, I didn't even consider the fact that I was one of the kids that had blown away.

There's a prevailing calm in Emmett as I leave the high school and drive back toward my parents' home. Ten years ago, I might have driven to Grandpa Wally's, but his farm is no longer in the family. Without any children or grandchildren able or willing to purchase the farmland, the family decided to sell it while I was in college.

The sale devastated me, though it's just one of many family

what is the exodus rate of variance?

farms sold, thanks in part to the mass exodus of young people from Idaho farms. In Fruitland, where I grew up, only 43 percent of children have stayed in their "commuting zone," according to the Opportunity Atlas, created by the U.S. Census Bureau to track social mobility.[1] Over in Emmett, where the family homestead is, 68 percent of the children who grew up there have stayed.[2] That's not a terrible exodus rate—in some areas of Idaho, the retention rate is as low as 20 percent.[3] But Emmett's commuting zone is not limited to this river valley: it extends throughout the entire Boise metropolitan area, which includes three large cities and has a population of more than seven hundred thousand people.[4] In reality, the percentage of Emmett natives staying in their "tract"—the region of the county where they grew up—is minuscule.[5] The number of children younger than eighteen living in Emmett continues to decline, and the town is "graying" with every year.[6] The town's prospects for future job growth and community vibrancy could literally die out.

Idaho is not the only place where this is happening. In their book, *Hollowing Out the Middle: The Rural Brain Drain and What It Means for America*, Patrick J. Carr and Maria J. Kefalas note that a "hemorrhaging of people, specifically the younger generation, is hollowing out many of the nation's small towns and rural communities."[7] In the early 2000s, Carr and Kefalas realized that the volume of loss was growing exponentially and that it "could spell the end of small-town America."[8]

The sorts of neighborly ties that once prompted us to care for one another have frayed. The oral history that helped us feel

connected to each other, and to the past, is dying out. The farmers that gave this land a sense of common work, purpose, and
culture are assailed on every side by economic consolidation,
suburban development, and brain drain. Without these shared
roots, we no longer appreciate our past or our ecology. We no
longer have a healthy, self-sufficient local economy. We no longer
share the seasons of feasting and harvesting that offered membership and meaning to this landscape.

Few Americans take easily to the idea of rootedness. Our
economists and politicians, teachers and celebrities often laud
mobility and progression over any sort of planted mentality. For
centuries, we have believed that success is a transitory thing, a
progression. We characterize achievement as inherently, etymo-
logically changeful: "You'll go far," we tell promising youth. Our
cultural touchstones, from Disney movies to pop songs, suggest
that separation, independence, and departure are inherent to true
triumph. Those who stay put—who take over the family business, say, or live in their hometown—are considered failures.

Consequently, there are people who believe the death of rural American towns is inevitable—perhaps even a sign of progress. Things like harvest festivals and decades-old mom-and-pop
businesses are nostalgic aspects of rural culture, often seen as su-
perfluous or secondary. Similarly, the loss of regional or local agriculture to large, industrialized farming is viewed as an inevitable
result of progress. To want anything different—to miss the small,
connected farms of yesteryear—is to wish for a "cutesy" relic of
the past.

But now, as I consider a future where most of Emmett's young

[handwritten margin note: mobility + progression v. rootedness/ planted mentality]

people have left, I fear not just the loss of family lore or tradition. I fear the loss of fruit that can come only from remaining in and loving our place. The children of Emmett who leave may indeed find success and happiness elsewhere. But, as we see from history, this kind of transience almost always results in extraction and exploitation of the places left behind.

Chapter Two

If you are to understand this valley, you must imagine it as it once was: full of life and diversity, with hundreds of small farming families working alongside each other. Imagine orchards next to crops, cows and hogs and chickens creating mayhem and plenitude in barnyard and kitchen. Imagine a land in which farmers put up hay together, raise barns together, and loan each other equipment and labor throughout each season—working not in isolation, but in tandem. The roots go down deep, connecting each part of this community to the land and to each other.

Now see its emptying: the slow homogenization of cropland, the aging farmer, the quiet Main Street. A farmer in this valley told me years ago that whenever he visited town, he no longer saw faces he recognized. He was beginning to feel like a stranger in his own community. The strands of communion and membership that once connected everyone have frayed, broken.

a true mariage

When I was a child, I remember walking the streets of my hometown with my parents and running into folks we knew. My mom had to budget extra time for every trip to Walmart, just for socializing. We shared countless connections with the people around us—with folks from the local sheriff and police departments, town hall and post office, churches and societies, farms and factories, hospitals and coffee shops. They all made us members of this small community, responsible for and accountable to each other.

But even then, things were changing. Local connections to the farm, in particular, were growing more feeble and sparse. The economy was struggling. Go back another generation, to when my dad was a kid growing up in Emmett, and the community was tighter-knit, the economy more vibrant. The farm crisis of the 1980s hadn't yet hit, and many hopeful young farmers were just getting started. My dad ate burgers with his mother at Roe-Ann's, a locally owned drive-in, after piano lessons in town, and played on the farm with his cousins after Sunday dinners. This community was full of connection and vitality. Exploitation and extraction hadn't yet taken their full toll.

To really understand how Emmett has changed and struggled, however, we have to look further than this. We have to rewind all the way to the town's beginning—back before people were driving up Freezeout Hill, out of this valley, and were descending into it instead. Back before people had anchored themselves in this soil, and everything was much like it is today: fluid, transient, unknown.

Emmett stretches along the banks of the Payette River, hedged in by dry mountain land. The foothills along its northern and southern edges, where two alluvial fans coalesce, always looked to me like a great set of knuckles pressed hard into the earth. Cottonwood trees lined the river, while big sagebrush and native grasses carpeted the hilltops and the lands below.[1] The big sagebrush sent their taproots three to thirteen feet down into the earth, anchoring them in the midst of their dry surroundings, lending their support to the soil. After a rainstorm, their leaves gave off a sweet, pungent aroma, filling the wide-open lands with fragrance. Purple mounds of lupine dotted the landscape, hugging the ground with their long roots and enriching the earth beneath with nitrogen.

Idaho historian Hiram Taylor French described this landscape as "a wide valley of virgin lands, fertile as those of the Nile, stretching invitingly on both sides of a copious stream," adding that it was perfectly calculated to "arrest the eye of the home seeker."[2] The Department of Commerce and Labor reported early on that the Snake River plateau boasted a sandy or silty loam derived from ancient lake beds, making the region "wonderfully fertile." Wherever farmers could bring water, the report's authors claimed, plants would grow.[3]

Members of the Shoshone and Bannock tribes often camped north of the Emmett Valley, long before pioneers began flocking to this part of Idaho. They were hunters and gatherers with a deep knowledge of the landscape's native plants and animals, terrain and climate. They traveled through the spring and summer, collecting and preserving food for use during winter: hunting wild game, fishing for salmon, and collecting native plants and roots such as the camas bulb in prairies to the north.

"Shoshones called the region between the Lower Boise River basin and the Weiser River Séhewoki'i, or 'the country where the willows are tied standing in line,'" author John W. Heaton documents. "They viewed Séhewoki'i as a 'land of abundance' where rivers teemed with fish and a variety of berries grew along the banks, such as the chokecherries that women mashed with a handheld grinding stone to make sun-dried patties. Hunters found small game and waterfowl there as well."[4]

In the early nineteenth century, fur trappers described this area of Idaho as "a landscape of grasses shoulder high to a horse, with brush and trees along even the intermittent streams and a riot of bird life," along with bison, antelope, sheep, elk, deer, beaver, grizzly bear, wolves, coyote, lynx, and cougar.[5]

Newcomers didn't start arriving here en masse until the 1800s—but after gold was found in the Boise Basin, hopeful wealth seekers from California and Oregon streamed into Idaho. They came with empty pockets and full ones, with their own mixture of hope and fear. They came for riches they could then bring elsewhere, ricocheting across the state at the mere mention of a gold strike. And so the Basin Trail and Umatilla-Placerville Road filled with horses and freight wagons, pack strings and stagecoaches, while others journeyed west from Fort Boise, braving the shifting sands of Freezeout Hill to reach the valley below.[6]

"They almost thought they could pick gold off the sagebrush," recalled Nellie Bane, who first came to this valley in 1883.[7] Idaho, the Gem State, is filled with the names that miners left behind. My hometown lies in the Treasure Valley, Emmett in Gem County. These miners were drawn by ancient stones, by the prospect of hope and wealth conjured out of old soil. All they had to do was dig.

Arid states were "settled and exploited by adventurous fortune-seekers who were precipitated upon the country in little more than a day by reported mineral discoveries within its boundaries," Ralph H. Hess wrote about the West in 1912. "All comers were competitors in robbing the land of such virgin wealth as was readily at hand."[8]

Idaho mountainsides are still pockmarked and scarred by the marks of mining, but most old mines in Idaho are now defunct: lost to memory and time, hidden in wild mountain land where people have forgotten their existence.[9] Ghost towns are scattered across the state, shells of hope and gold lust, weathered buildings turning gray and decaying as nature takes back its ground. Silver City is one such ghost town in the south, Pearl another just east of Emmett.

Emmett was founded almost accidentally by two men who had left their homes behind. Nathaniel Martin and Jonathan Smith joined a wagon train from Missouri to Oregon in hopes of finding their own fortune. But when the two camped in the Emmett Valley, under the shade of the cottonwood trees that clustered along the Payette River, they decided they had found their place. They built a ferry at the junction of the Umatilla and Placerville stage roads, along a space of the Payette River that often

were the travelers mormon?
did they come of H. louis - the gd away city to the west?

proved treacherous when waters ran high in the spring. The land they homesteaded became known as "the Smith and Martin Ranch."[10] Jonathan Smith dug the valley's first irrigation ditch in the 1870s and planted a garden full of fruit trees, berry bushes, and grapevines.

At first, the valley was home to only a handful of pioneers. Here, they built homesteads, hostelries, and feed barns. But as traffic through the area blossomed and the promise of irrigation beckoned, the settlement became an attractive location for a handful of enterprising townspeople. Emmett's first sawmill was constructed in 1870 by John F. Basye and his son-in-law, Samuel Walker.[11] Their enterprise was soon followed by a gristmill and a general store.

In those early days, the village of Emmett was full of lawlessness and violence. The history of Emmett (originally known as Emmettsville) is rife with horrific stories of murder and abuse of local Native Americans, who were subjected to blatant racism by newcomers to the valley.[12] Entire tribes were slaughtered by drunken trappers and miners, and war constantly loomed on the horizon. In the mid-1800s, the Emmett Valley was also home to Pickett's Corral: a notorious rendezvous for highwaymen, horse thieves, and hawkers of bogus gold dust.[13] There are multiple tales of drunkenness, angry brawls, and shootings stemming from this time. The town's early population of journeying miners, wayfarers, and loggers didn't lend itself to sobriety, community, or respect. Most came and went without families or roots. Emmett was a stopping place en route to treasure elsewhere.

There were three saloons in the town before there was a single church building.[14]

⚶

Pulitzer Prize–winning author Wallace Stegner once called the United States' two archetypal populations the "boomers" and the "stickers," and argued that our country has since been populated— torn apart and rebuilt, repeatedly—by these two groups in various guises.[15] This is especially true in the West, the land both he and I grew up in.

Stickers are those who settle down and invest. Boomers come to extract value from a place and then leave. Since the mid-nineteenth century, there have been more boomers than stickers in Idaho's history. "Deeply lived-in places are exceptions rather than the rule in the West," Stegner wrote in his collection of essays *Where the Bluebird Sings to the Lemonade Springs*. "For one thing, all western places are new; for another, many of the people who established them came to pillage, or to work for pillagers, rather than to settle for life. When the pillaging was done or the dream exploded, they moved on, to be replaced in the next boom by others just as hopeful and just as footloose."[16]

This trend toward transience, it must be noted, has birthed a nation filled with innovation and incredible success stories. The American Dream is, in essence, about economic and class transience: the ability to move from poverty to wealth, from lack to abundance. This is part of our legacy, one oft touted and celebrated by politician and writer alike. But it's only when people decide to stay that a place can develop.

The transience in Emmett's early days wasn't always because of an interest in moving on, however. Often, prejudice and bigotry prevented those who wanted to settle down from putting down roots. In the race for conquest that characterizes so much of the West's early history, things were not easy for Idaho's migrant population, especially for minorities who wanted to live and work here.

Although many black men, women, and families came to Idaho in search of economic opportunity, they faced intimidation and discrimination once they arrived. In 1863, Boise County passed a law that excluded black and Chinese locals from prospecting, and the territorial legislature introduced a bill in 1865 that aimed to prohibit black migration to the region.[17] There were fewer than a dozen African American–owned farms in Idaho in the early twentieth century, and that number would dwindle in coming decades as the children of farm owners migrated to cities in pursuit of better jobs and less social isolation.[18]

By 1870, Chinese immigrants made up more than one-quarter of the state's total non-Indian population—and a decade later, the ratio of Asians to whites in Idaho was higher than in any other territory or state in the United States.[19] But Chinese miners were subject to rampant racism and violence when they traveled here searching for gold and consequently suffered the injustices of discriminatory legislation, such as a monthly tax on all Chinese residents of Idaho.[20] Chinese immigrants once cultivated produce farms and opened restaurants to feed Idaho's mining population

and towns, and built neighborhoods and communities for themselves across the state. But in the face of racism and discrimination,
many chose to leave. Several of the settlements where Chinese
immigrants lived, tended gardens, and made food for their neighbors have disappeared.

Along with its indigenous and migrant populations, Idaho's
resources were also severely exploited and abused during this
era. In the West, immense natural resources nurtured the assumption that we could achieve limitless growth, expansion,
and wealth. Each new boom led to intense surges of extraction
as a result—predicated on the assumption that there would be no
real consequences to our pillaging.

Trappers nearly destroyed the state's beaver population over
the course of a few decades.[21] During the gold rush, miners
stripped away entire mountainsides via hydraulic mining, leaving heaps of rubble in their wake.[22] Loggers began decimating
white pine and conifer forests across the Midwest and Northwest.[23] Idaho has always offered plenty to its inhabitants. But as
long as westerners have known about its bounty, they've done
their best to use it for their own gain.

Boomers and exploiters didn't "stick" when the going got
tough. In the late 1800s, many of the land's original gold seekers
and settlers began experiencing hard times and moved back East.
The gold boom finally hit its bust. People exhausted the land's
long-held riches, then abandoned it. Emmett's little newspaper,
the *Emmett Messenger-Index*, wrote of the many migrants passing
through the valley on their way back home. They were "going
back to their wives' people," wrote the paper's editor, "and when

they get back will probably wish they had stayed where they were. This hunting for good times in these days is an uphill business. Times are always better just a little further on, but they are better in Idaho than any place we know of."[24]

Idaho settlers slowly began to change in population and kind, and with them, behaviors regarding the land shifted toward permanence.

One such group came from much farther away than the East Coast. During the early 1900s, Japanese immigrants came to work on farms and in refineries throughout the Snake River Valley.[25]

Hajimu Fujii was one of the earliest Japanese immigrants to settle down in Emmett. As a young man, he was determined to become a farmer in America. He grew up on a rice and silkworm farm in Tottori Prefecture, Japan, but began planning to immigrate to America while still in high school.[26] He and a classmate named Katsuji Hashitani traveled from Seattle to Billings, Montana, where they worked thinning sugar beets.

The work was miserable. "Nothing could compare with this back-breaking, literally stoop labor, which tossed them into their bunks at night in utter exhaustion," Hashitani's daughter Alice wrote later in a retrospective on her father's life.[27] Eager for a better way to make a living, Hashitani and Fujii left the sugar beet farm in Billings and traveled to Missoula, Montana, where they joined a section gang and kept ten miles of track in repair. They struggled with the hardship and grueling labor, the lack of hope that America offered them during those years—but her father "trusted in God and His will for his life," Alice says.[28]

Japanese internment
↑ was located in Idaho
with WW2

After two years, Hashitani and Fujii found themselves in Emmett, where they pooled their resources and bought a team of horses, a wagon, and a buggy. They rented eighty acres and began planting fruits and vegetables in the earth, transporting the fruit of their labor to Emmett, Pearl, Idaho City, and Placerville.[29] But soon after, the Idaho State Legislature introduced an "alien land law" that banned Asian immigrants from landownership. This law was one of several passed in western states—including California, Oregon, Utah, Montana, Wyoming, and Texas—generated by anti-Chinese and anti-Japanese sentiment. These laws would not be ruled unconstitutional until 1952.[30] —➔ *holy shit*

After Fujii married and had children of his own, he figured out a way around Idaho's alien land law: he purchased forty acres in his children's names, since they were by birth natural citizens of Idaho. Fujii never stopped fighting alien land laws, partnering with the Japanese Association of Western Idaho (JAWI) to fight for the rights of Japanese immigrants. Voluntary associations such as JAWI, writes historian Eric Walz, "created social and economic connections within the community, protected their common interests against those seeking to exploit them, and, as they developed a greater sense of permanence, provided avenues through which they could interact with the host society."[31]

Along with the Japanese, another group was ready to settle in Idaho. Starting in the mid-nineteenth century, members of the Church of Jesus Christ of Latter-day Saints began sending pioneers north from Utah, where they settled throughout southern Idaho, hoping to expand their earthly kingdom of God. The

Latter-day Saints found their way to Emmett around 1900 and increased over a hundredfold by the 1930s.[32] Today, Idaho has the second-largest Mormon population in the world.[33]

Many of the other farming families that began flocking to Emmett around the turn of the century were immigrants from the Great Plains: poor families trying to find a piece of the American Dream, seeking a community where they could build a new life for their families—a place where they could settle for good.

As they began grubbing sagebrush and studying the soil beneath, preparing it for planting, they would have found that the western Emmett Valley had a high water table, as well as an accumulation of soluble salts and alkali, that made farming difficult.[34] But cropland to the east of Emmett, on "the bench" (a mesa to the north), in the valleys of Montour, Sweet, and Ola, as well as along Black Canyon, proved to contain the rich loam that farmers were looking for. Some of the soil had a hardpan layer, but much of the landscape was ideally situated for the planting of corn, alfalfa, small grain, and pasture crops. All they needed, they surmised, was the water.

Choosing to stick, even in a place with good soil, demanded tremendous effort. Rainfall was not enough to supply farmers with the water they need, and intense work was necessary to provide irrigation. The first canal in the region was the Last Chance Canal, which ran along the eastern side of the valley and provided more than six thousand inches of water to the valley's aspiring farmers in east Emmett.[35] In the 1890s, construction in the Emmett Valley began on the Farmer's Co-op Canal, which was forty miles long upon completion.[36]

Preparing the ground was even more work. After clearing sagebrush, enterprising orchardists would plow, level, and harrow the ground. Then they would drag joiners over the earth to "work it down," making it smooth and level.[37] Irl Bishop recalled clearing land for the Idaho Orchard Company in those early days: "The dust flew in every direction; the drivers and horses were covered with dirt. It took two months to get the ground ready."[38]

Once the land had been cleared, Emmett's settlers began planting a crop that makes sense only if you plan to stay: trees. The valley seemed perfect for fruit farming. On the slopes to the south and east of Emmett, the sandy loam went seven feet down, providing excellent drainage, and the elevation kept orchards a few degrees warmer than the valley floor.

Emmett's first orchard was planted around 1871, and it flourished.[39] In 1908, J. R. Field—considered the region's finest horticulturist at the time—planted the valley's first cherry orchard after purchasing 250 acres on the east slope.[40] Over the next several decades, plum, cherry, peach, and apple trees spread throughout the valley. The state produced 924,000 bushels of fruit in 1909, fruit that became known throughout the world for its quality.[41] Field wrote in a paper on fruit growing in the Payette Valley that "the market[s] for Idaho fruits are worldwide":

The Italian prune, shipped fresh and sold as a plum, goes to London and other foreign ports. Apples, to the orient and Australia, and the bulk of the fruit is sold to the great markets of the East. Here, where nature provides the richest of soils, long periods of sunshine, and flowing streams, man has only to divert the water to the willing soil to produce fruit of high quality and fine appearance which is the envy of the eastern fruit growers.[42]

By the beginning of the twentieth century, Emmett was so well-known for its prune shipments, its baseball team was known as the Prune Pickers.[43]

The town was incorporated in 1900 and became home to a city hall and fire department, as well as several churches. Captain James Gunn, editor of the *Boise Sentinel*, described Emmett thus in his 1893 article "A Trip to Emmett": "With the river winding through it, fringed with foliage, and the town of Emmett nestling in the distance, perhaps no more peaceful, quiet, and beautiful scene can be witnessed anywhere in the mountain regions. . . . Not only fruit, but almost anything that can be grown in a temperate zone, thrives here."[44]

The arrival of the Payette Valley Railroad, called the Pumpkin Vine by locals, contributed further to the settling down, connecting the people of Emmett to the sustenance of outside commerce and potential settlers.[45]

As the *Emmett Messenger-Index*'s editor wrote, "With the arrival of the railroad all realized that our bands of isolation are broken and now it is a fair field and no favors. . . . The month of March, 1902, is a red letter month for Emmett, and henceforth Emmett people will date events from the day the railroad came."[46]

Emmett's population grew from three hundred to one thousand in just two years, and it gained a city hall, cement sidewalks, electric lights, telephone lines, water works, and a sewer system. To Emmett's townspeople, the railroad meant growth, prosperity, greater stability, and connection to the necessary lifeblood of trade.

The train helped bring Andy Little to Emmett—and with him, generations of new families and workers who would stick in this town. A Scottish immigrant, Little arrived in Idaho accompanied by two faithful sheepdogs named Katie and Jim. Unable to make a living on his father's farm in Scotland, he had immigrated to America, arriving in Emmett with two dollars in his pocket.[47] He started working for a fellow Scotsman, Robert Aikman, on his sheep ranch outside Emmett, herding a band of about twelve hundred ewes along Willow Creek. Andy was hardworking and intelligent, and Aikman was impressed with his work ethic. At the end of Andy's first year, Aikman told him he had earned enough salary to buy half a band of sheep. He offered Andy the money or the sheep.

"If you take the sheep," Aikman added, "I will sell the other half on a note and you will have your first band."

At first, Andy was unsure. He nearly took the salary to use it to go back to Scotland. But he was excited about this river valley and eager to see its business prospects grow. After some deliberation, Andy took the sheep and began his career in Emmett—one that blossomed until Andy became known as the Sheep King of Idaho. At its height, Andy's flock numbered upward of 120,000, which he ranged over seven counties.[48] During the summers, the sheep were ranged in Idaho's national forests to the north. When

bleat – wavering cry

they were brought down from the mountains each autumn, the bleating of ewes and lambs could be heard for miles around.[49]

Andy chose to live and work in the Emmett Valley because he saw in it the same neighborliness and village closeness he grew up with in Scotland. Emmett had sprung from a neglected outpost into a community that many—Andy included—saw as a potential garden of plenty. But it still needed investment: needed people to embed their talents, hopes, and resources in the soil. Thankfully, Andy's family loved participating in Emmett's rhythms and life. According to author Louise Shadduck, Adis Little (the matriarch of the family, also an immigrant from Scotland) enjoyed watching movies at the little Emmett theater. Admission was six cents, and local piano player Josie Russell provided the films' background music. On the theater's opening night in 1910, owner Fred Larkin handed out a booklet that told townspeople, "Parents, with babies in arms, are especially invited, as we love babies."[50] Adis loved to knit in the dark theater, and family members often bragged that she could watch an entire movie without looking down at her knitting needles and never drop a stitch.

The Littles were major employers in the Emmett area. They owned more than six thousand acres throughout the Payette and Boise Valleys, and employed as many as four hundred workers: their sheep empire required a number of shearers, herders, cooks, and camp tenders, all spread across the twenty-seven ranches they owned and managed. The supplies necessary to house, feed, and clothe all these employees were an economic boon for Emmett businesses.

Every spring, Emmett's hills were covered with bands of

sheep, and throughout the lambing season "it looked like the hills were alight with fireflies as the herders' lanterns gleamed and moved about in the darkness," author Ruth Lyon writes.[51] Shearing time was an occasion for fiddling, feasting, and the entertainment of "sheep poets."[52] In 1931, the Idaho Wool Growers Association reported that Andy's wool clip was equal to approximately eight hundred thousand pounds from ninety-two thousand clips.[53]

Andy was a rigorous employer: he didn't allow gambling or drinking on his ranches and often required his workers to put in twelve-hour workdays. But Shadduck notes that Andy usually put in fourteen to sixteen hours of labor himself. Most of his employees found him to be fair, honest, and good-natured.

Andy encouraged more immigrants to put down roots in this valley: many of his shepherds were Basque immigrants who traveled to this area from their homeland in northern Spain. To this day, Idaho has one of the largest Basque populations in the United States.[54] Peruvian immigrants were also hired by several local sheepherding companies, respected for both their work ethic and expertise. Herders spent much of their time alone, out in wild Idaho mountain land, with their bands of sheep. Many of them traveled with a crock of sourdough starter they used to make homemade biscuits over the campfire.

After his family had lived and worked in the Emmett Valley for some time, Andy built a sixty-four-hundred-square-foot home entirely out of reinforced concrete on the outskirts of Emmett. The walls are a foot thick. Andy was terrified of earthquakes after reading extensively about the San Francisco earthquake of

[handwritten margin note: Boise has a basque influence as well as Cn r stuuidad was a Shepard from peru]

1906, and so he built this home to withstand the worst Mother Nature might throw at it. When the house was complete, Andy surveyed it with pride. "No earthquake could ever take this down," he said.[55]

The Little family decided to call it the "Forever House."

Chapter Three

My own ancestors were not rich when they came to this river valley. Walter Sisler—my great-great-great-grandfather—was a tall, good-looking man with dark hair and a determined face. Leanna Sisler wore her hair in a tight bun at the nape of her neck, hair parted straight down the middle. She lost two babies to sickness before she set foot in Idaho, both before they were two years old. The Sislers had tried farming in a few other places before they came to Idaho, in addition to picking up some handyman and painting jobs. But, inevitably, the family would pull up stakes and move on—seeking something they could not find in Kansas or the Dakotas.

Around the turn of the century, advertisements for agricultural land in Idaho caught the Sislers' attention. I found one brochure from the era that predicted Emmett, at the time a community of twenty-five hundred residents, would soon be twenty-five thousand residents strong and a "Garden of Eden." Tired of a life of transience, of enduring brutal winters and bare cupboards while moving from town to town across the Great Plains, Walter and Leanna decided to try settling down for good in Idaho.

Along with some other relatives from Kansas who had the "Idaho fever," Walter Sisler traveled to Idaho and began developing a forty-acre farm from the sagebrush outside New Plymouth, just a few miles west of Emmett. Leanna and their three older children followed him out by train. They planted hay and grain and planned to put in acres of trees the next year.

Those early years were not easy. "The first winter in Idaho was a very wet one, with almost nothing that could be called a road," Warren Sisler, Walter's youngest son, chronicled later. Family members who had followed Walter and Leanna to Idaho wore out. "The hardships of hauling feed and general travel, and clearing the land and building, began to wear on them and they became discouraged," Warren said. They all moved back except Walter and Leanna, who, Warren says, "were forced by circumstances to stay."

Warren doesn't say which circumstances prompted the Sislers to remain. Perhaps it was because Warren himself, who had been born shortly after Walter and Leanna arrived in Idaho, was very sickly for the first decade of his life. Leanna and Walter struggled with illness, too, in those early days. Perhaps they stayed because they were putting down roots: Walter and Leanna's eldest daughter, my great-great-grandmother Alta, married local farmer Robert Howard in 1908. Whatever the reason, the Sislers became stickers.

the history of empty dentistry

Robert Howard came to Emmett with his parents, Allen and Ida, and his three siblings: Millie, Ben, and Gladys. Allen was a traveling dentist from Minnesota with a thick mustache and inquisitive eyes. Although he had received a good education, dentistry did not pay well, so he traveled about Idaho by horseback, doing dental work, often journeying up north to work in mining towns, carrying a small foldable dentist chair and set of instruments. Poor miners often gave him chickens in exchange for a tooth extraction. Ida, meanwhile, taught at two Emmett schoolhouses, and the couple's children all helped on the family farm.

Robert (fondly known as Bob or RJ) began farming with his in-laws after he married Alta. The Sislers moved from New Plymouth to the outskirts of Emmett in 1916, and Walter started an eighty-acre apple orchard.

"The valley is a fertile district," he wrote. "It is well adapted to fruit growing and has about fifty thousand acres of irrigated land; at least half of which would be very good for the growing of apples and prunes, if the industry could be made to pay."

But making a profit on an orchard wasn't always easy. Although the fruit was popular and grew well, shipping costs took a toll on farmers' proceeds, and the fruit market itself was often unstable from year to year. Production costs could also be a burden: the codling moth and other insect infestations often plagued fruit farmers' bottom line. Walter, Leanna, and their sons often traveled back to Nebraska to peddle their fruit, hoping to make some money.

"Bob and Papa and Warren are all out on the road with apples," Leanna wrote to daughter Alta in a December 1926 letter from West Point, Nebraska. "The days sure get long. I don't know how long we will be here. I think they must have near 200 baskets on hand yet."

By this point, Bob and Alta had seven children. Frances was the oldest, born in 1909. Alta gave birth to my Grandpa Dad—named Walter Allen in honor of his two grandfathers—in 1911. Grandpa Dad started digging irrigation ditches for his family's 160-acre farm when he was nine or ten years old. Bob taught him some irrigation tricks and ideas he had tinkered with over the course of his farming career, in hopes that they would be able to keep their farm in good health.

The Howards and Sislers worked hard. But poverty haunts and pervades many of the letters Leanna wrote to Alta, like a seeping cold. Things were not easy. She could only hope they would get better. In the meantime, they kept working. In another December 1926 letter—this time from Wayne, Nebraska—Leanna wrote, "Apple selling is a bad job here. So many people got hit with cheap bulk apples, that they are afraid to take hold. . . . Papa said he hired an old man to help sell apples. He is going up and down the streets, shouting 'Idaho apples for sale.'"

"My operation of the orchard from 1922 to 1926 has not been profitable," Walter Sisler later admitted in a letter of his own. "Some years I managed to make a little over my expenses—taken as a whole I have about broke even, without receiving any interest on my investment in the orchard." He found that his average gain in good years was only one and a half cents per box.

But Walter persisted in cultivating his orchard. In a letter from November 1935, almost a decade later, it becomes clear that although old age was beginning to wear on Leanna and Walter, they were still dedicated to their farm. They had Bob and Alta to help them, and the old and the young worked together to make ends meet.

"Papa's eyes are getting worse all the time," Leanna wrote to Warren, who was living in Seattle at the time. "He has been overseeing the apple drying all fall. They have over 2,600 pounds dried. They have been at it 45 days without missing a day except Sunday. I expect you have seen in the papers about freezing weather we are having; the first hard freeze came about two weeks ago. Had about two car loads of apples on the trees yet. They got them off before they were hurt very bad, but a lot of the culls that were outside froze till they can't use them anymore." Leanna notes later on in her letter that an estimated ten thousand carloads of apples were ruined in "the three northwest states" (Idaho, Oregon, and Washington) that year.

Despite these challenges, however, there's a growth of fellowship and camaraderie in Leanna's letters: she shares neighborhood news, including church functions, baptisms, and marriages. Amid the struggles of pioneer life, it appears that community was blossoming. I have a picture of Walter and Leanna from those days, sitting outside their little farmhouse in Emmett: Leanna is wearing a long calico dress and round spectacles, her white hair pulled back in that same prim bun. Walter still looks lanky and strong from farmwork; he's holding his great-granddaughter Helen on his lap. They look happy and comfortable. They look as if they have finally found their place.

⁂

Staying in the place they cultivated would be more challenging than they'd expect. By the time Bob and Alta's son—my Grandpa Dad—was an adult, the family, along with all their neighbors, were facing both the Great Depression and the Dust Bowl.

Grandpa Dad had been raised to have grit. When he was thirteen, he went on a two-day journey by himself from Boise to the family farm on the Emmett mesa, or "the bench." It was at least a thirty-five-mile journey. He lit a fire, ate in the quiet, and stared up at the stars. The journey could be dangerous and lonely; there were cougars about in the wild, open land. But Grandpa Dad felt safe on his beloved horse's back. He could handle a four-horse team by the time he was eight, and he still worked with teams long after most farmers had dispensed with keeping them about the farm. His favorite horse was named Sweetheart.

All the years he kept the farm going while his father was gone had irrevocably shaped his character. Most farmers are independent, often stubborn. But Grandpa Dad carried an immense burden of responsibility from a very young age. While his brothers played sports, he kept to the farm and developed into the sort of young man who loved exploring the wilderness of Idaho's deserted foothills by himself, exhibiting both a fierce self-sufficiency and a deep passion for farming.

After graduating from Emmett High School, Grandpa Dad attended Northwest Nazarene College (now Northwest Nazarene University) in Nampa, Idaho, about thirty-five miles from the family farm. But he never finished. It's somewhat unclear why: My great-aunt Helen told me her father went back to the farm so that his younger brothers could have their chance to go to school and pursue sports. His son later said that Grandpa Dad knew he wanted to be on the farm. No degree seemed necessary to prepare him for work he had already done his whole life.

There's another reason Grandpa Dad left college, however. At college, he met Iva—a lovely, dark-haired girl with a beautiful singing voice—and he was determined to marry her. So he headed back to the Emmett bench, resolving to save his money and try to procure a farm of his own.

My great-grandmother, Iva Ax—otherwise known as Grandma Mom—came to Idaho from Nortonville, North Dakota. Her parents were immigrants from Denmark and Sweden who met and married in North Dakota, where they had four children. Iva, the baby of the family, was feisty, determined, and talented. She wanted to go to college and pursue music, but "things were hard up," as Grandpa Dad once put it. After graduating from high school, she got a teaching certificate and taught at the little one-room schoolhouse near her parents' farm. When she applied to the Northwest Nazarene College two years later, she asked her parents to sell the farm and go with her. They'd had three years of failure there on the farm, plagued by drought and hail. The Depression and Dust Bowl were affecting families all throughout the Midwest by this point.

Iva convinced her parents to move with her to Nampa—over eleven hundred miles away from their home on the plains. Her parents, along with two of her brothers and her sister-in-law, packed all their worldly possessions into a 1930s automobile and left behind their lives.

"Iva, not putting any of them down, but she was the leader of the family," Grandpa Dad once said. One of my dad's cousins told me that Grandma Mom was "the glue" that kept her family close.

Idaho offered a new beginning to the Ax family. But things weren't much better in the Treasure Valley when they arrived. Next to Montana, Idaho had the highest rate of emigration of any western state in the 1920s. If the state's first bust came in the late 1800s as the gold boom was dying down, its second arrived amid the difficulties of the Great Depression.[1] The state was ravaged by drought in the 1930s, with 1934 crop losses estimated at $22.4 million. In 1932, the price of wheat dropped to 29 cents a bushel, and prices for Idaho's "famous potatoes" fell to 10 cents a sack.[2] In some counties, unemployed workers deliberately set forest fires so they would get hired to fight them. Family incomes in the state dropped by as much as 50 percent, and many lost their farms to local land banks.

Yet despite the hardship they would face in the Northwest, folks from Oklahoma and Arkansas were constantly moving to Idaho at this time, "headed for greener pastures," as reporter Syd Albright wrote in an article for a Coeur d'Alene newspaper.[3]

During these years, Walter and Leanna Sisler divided their barn and silo into little apartments and offered them to local families in need of shelter. Leonard J. Arrington, a Mormon

40

historian who chronicled at length the early life of the state's farmers, wrote that when the Great Depression hit Idaho with full force, neighborliness and community helped keep many local farmers afloat:

> Sometime during the winter of 1932–1933 a family acquaintance was foreclosed by his creditor, and a sheriff's sale ordered for a certain Monday. All the farmers in his neighborhood gathered together on Sunday evening and agreed upon a plan to help their friend. They would attend the sale and refuse to bid against each other. The next day, as the auctioneer went through his accustomed chant, a splendid team of horses sold for $1.50; a grain binder, $2.00; a hay mover, $1.00. Prices of other animals and equipment ran from a low of 50 cents to a high of $3.00. The farmers duly paid the sums they had bid, received the items purchased, and promptly turned them back to the farmer who had been foreclosed.[4]

It was a tough time to start farming, but Grandpa Dad was determined. His grandfather had offered to loan him some land on a share-crop arrangement so he could get his start. His parents lived just down the road. And Iva was a farm girl, with the talent and grit to help him build a life from the soil. They were both smart and hardworking. Together, they knew they could make it.

Grandpa Dad and Grandma Mom had less than five dollars in their pockets when they moved into their first farmhouse. Alta split her spices with her new daughter-in-law, so that the couple had something to cook with. Walter Sisler owed Grandpa Dad some money for labor on the farm, but couldn't afford to pay him the monthly forty-dollar wages. Instead, he offered his grandson a team of horses in payment. Grandpa Dad dug through some piles of scrap lumber to find boards for fencing and fixed up a broken-down plow so that he didn't have to buy a new one. He borrowed a grain drill from one neighbor. Another neighbor offered him hay for free. Yet another loaned Grandpa Dad his first five head of milk cows.[5] They were lean years—but somehow, like the Gospel story of the loaves and fishes, they always had enough. Every morning, Grandma Mom woke at the crack of dawn and milked the cows. The couple skimmed the cream off the top, hauled it into town, and sold it to a local creamery. The milk cows covered their operating costs, and the steers in the feedlot took care of their land payments. Grandpa Dad generally grew field corn—sometimes called cow corn because it's used for cattle feed—as well as alfalfa, sugar beets, and sweet corn in his fields. He used the field corn and alfalfa to feed his livestock, and his sweet corn went to Emmett's cannery.

Grandpa Dad and Grandma Mom were too poor to buy a clock or timepiece back in those days. But the Paytons, an elderly couple who lived next door to them, went about their lives with painstaking precision. So every day, Grandma Mom kept an eye on Mr. Payton while he worked in the fields. When he straightened up and went inside, she knew it was noon. She then ran outside and hung a white dish towel from the fence, signaling to Grandpa Dad that it was lunchtime.

Eventually, the couple saved up enough money to purchase

feed corn = cattle corn

what if the Federal land bank?

some land of their own and bought their first eighty acres from the Federal Land Bank.

During the winters, Grandpa Dad helped build roads in Emmett and worked with fellow laborers on the Black Canyon Reservoir. Grandma Mom, meanwhile, grew almost everything the couple ate. She milked the cows, cared for the chickens, and tended a huge vegetable garden. She canned and preserved garden produce and butchered chickens most mornings for lunch and dinner. With continuous effort and hard labor, they managed to stay within their means—even save some extra and get ahead—despite the economic woe surrounding them.

Grandpa Dad and Grandma Mom had three children: Helen, Walter Jr. (my grandfather, known as Wally), and Charles Eldon (known as Ed). Grandpa Wally looks remarkably like his mother—he has her mirthful eyes, dark hair, and strong jaw. He also inherited her singing voice, her exuberant joy. As a young man, he would waltz around the kitchen with his mother, the two of them laughing and singing.

Great-Aunt Helen looks like her father in many ways: she has the same narrow face, the same thoughtful expression. She was a beautiful, quiet girl who loved helping Iva around the house. She remembers sitting in the kitchen with her mother, towels on their laps, shelling a bushel of fresh peas or snapping green beans from the garden in the summer. Helen helped Grandma Mom cook lunch feasts for the hay men and threshers during the harvest, often feeding as many as twelve to fourteen workers at a time. They worked side by side in the tiny farmhouse kitchen, frying chicken, mashing potatoes, and baking pies. To this day,

↓ Same with day job / spreading the household meal

although she is in her late eighties, Helen still gathers fresh fruit and berries from her garden and makes pies for family and friends, using her mother's recipes.

In the evenings, Grandma Mom sat at the old upright piano in the living room and sang hymns with Grandpa Wally. Even though she never finished her degree in music, Grandma Mom sang for many a wedding and funeral in Emmett. At least a couple of times, a pastor asked her to sing at the last minute—so Grandma Mom dashed to the church with her apron on, covered in flour, and sang behind a screen so folks couldn't see her disheveled appearance.

I never met Grandma Mom, but I grew up hearing stories about her, eating desserts carefully copied from her handwritten recipes, listening to her favorite hymns. Her presence wafted through our lives long after she herself was gone. Both Grandma Mom and Grandpa Dad passed down many simple treasures: lines of recipes and poems, stories and songs they had committed to heart. Those lines formed a pattern and pulse we could all follow. The dust and decay of farm life was strong: all those butchered chickens, the stench of manure, the slicing pain of a tired back. My great-grandparents always used to remind folks, "Better a death in the barn than in the house," because they had experienced both. But they shared the treasures that filled their lives with joy. And so decades after she traveled out West with her parents, after she married Grandpa Dad in a quiet Nampa church and waltzed around a farmhouse kitchen, Grandma Mom continued to serve as the glue that helped hold together the people and the places she loved.

Before Grandpa Dad died in 2007, I remember my sister, Katie, and I drove out to visit him with our parents, and we played his favorite hymns for him. I pulled out my violin and tuned it as Grandpa Dad watched me with shining eyes. He was using an oxygen tank at this point and looked more frail than I'd ever seen him. Katie sat down at the old upright piano where Grandma Mom had sat so many years before. Then we began to play "Amazing Grace," followed by "I Come to the Garden Alone," an old Methodist hymn that Grandma Mom had loved. Grandpa Dad closed his eyes and listened with a soft smile on his face. Before we hugged him goodbye, he recited several favorite poems and Scripture verses and showed us Grandma Mom's love notes one more time. He repeated his now-familiar tales of childhood, of a lifetime of love, of a happy farm town.

By the time he passed away, Grandpa Dad, the consummate sticker, had worn tracks in the farmhouse's old green carpet: from the bedroom to the sink and fridge, from the fridge to the little kitchen table, from the table to his beloved La-Z-Boy chair and television. After Grandma Mom died, his rhythms and patterns rarely altered. His life settled into a cadence and ritual that persisted on, year after year. He knew all his neighbors, and they knew him. He was out riding his tractor until his early nineties, attending church services and teaching Sunday school until the end of his days.

His siblings left the farm and traveled the world, but Grandpa Dad stayed on the bench, next to his parents and grandparents, carrying on their farmland, traditions, and way of life, for ninety-six years. Those carpet trails aptly describe Grandpa Dad: he was too stubborn and thrifty to replace old green carpet, too stuck in his ways to alter his footfalls, too heartsick over the loss of his wife to alter one jot or tittle of her decor. But most of all, Grandpa Dad was too in love with the place to ever leave. He kept up his lonely vigil from barn to field, field to house, house to church, and back again, long after his contemporaries had left, been bought out, or passed away. He was still wearing trails in the carpet, the soil, the roads—growing in wisdom and knowledge as each season passed in his place, as new growth sprang up underneath his feet.

Grandpa Dad may have worn tracks in the carpet, but he did not stay in Emmett because he was stuck or because it was easy. As a girl, I did not understand the importance of his quiet constancy, nor did I understand the effort it required. Now, as I look back at what's been lost and seek to understand the forces that shape Emmett, I recognize what Grandpa Dad was up against.

This valley's transformation over the past two centuries has not been the benign work of an invisible hand. It was the result of deliberate choices to maximize profit rather than embrace limits, to prioritize "progress" over rootedness. Grandpa Dad stood against those choices and made a "Forever House" despite them. I wonder if I can too.

Chapter Four

W hile in college, I started working for the admissions department, giving campus tours to prospective students and their families. On one particular tour, as soon as I said that I had grown up in Idaho, I saw the prospective student's mother lean toward her husband.

"So it does exist," she whispered with a soft smirk.

When she saw that I had overheard, she blushed and explained. The family's pastor did not believe Idaho was real. He told them the state was "made up by the federal government," part of a scheme to get more tax dollars.

"After all," he would say with a laugh, "who's ever met someone from Idaho?"

Well, they met me—making this the first (and last) time I've smashed a conspiracy theory by my very existence. But that rather strange family stirred something inside me: a growing frustration, I think, over how hard it was to justify a place that nobody knew anything about.

This wasn't the first time I had experienced cluelessness when my home state came up in conversations. Idaho was a place sparsely populated enough, it seemed, to foster both silly stereotypes and complete ignorance. Sometimes, I just leaned into the stereotypes. When one classmate asked me about Idaho potatoes, I jestingly told her that I grew up in a house surrounded by potato fields, with an outhouse in the backyard and no paved roads for miles. She believed me.

I saw other friends from rural states struggle with this: the incredulity we all felt when Iowa, Ohio, and Idaho morphed into a featureless blob in the imaginations of our peers. The names are similar, in their defense. But sometimes, it felt as if places with farmers and cows and corn were all the same to people who hadn't lived there. The few folks I talked to who had traveled through Idaho on road trips told me how surprised they were to discover its beauty. I was not sure what they expected—83,600 square feet of brown fields, perhaps?

Us rural kids adapted pretty quickly. We got used to telling or hearing jokes about our hometowns, embraced the derision and amusement of people who were cool enough to come from places like Chicago or Los Angeles. One of my friends said she was from the "Middle of Nowhere, Indiana" for so long, it took me years to learn the name of her actual hometown.

Later, at happy hours, banquets, and lunches in Washington, DC, I was often introduced as the person from Idaho, the person whose grandfathers were farmers. The novelty of my farming roots made little sense to me at first. Now, however, I know that less than 2 percent of Americans work on a farm these days. Very few of us still have direct ties to the land and to those who work

[handwritten note: Judge a place by profit & utility]

it. My childhood in rural Idaho gave me a connection to the land and to our food system that many folks in DC had not experienced.

In one sense, this ignorance was harmless. In another sense, it was indicative of a political and economic system that judges places not by how well they serve their own inhabitants, or by the culture and people they keep in place, but by their profit and utility.

Some cities may be exceptions: places like New York City, which are so iconic in their own right they're viewed as intrinsically valuable. But many rural towns are considered interchangeable and expendable, valuable not for their own sake but because their resources—lumber, paper, coal, minerals, gemstones, oil, gas, produce, dairy, meat, and grains, to name a few—have for many decades been exported to other places by large corporations. These *[handwritten note: a stock]* towns' worth (or lack thereof) is contingent on what other spaces think of them, take from them, or offer them. This extraction of worth, hope, and resources is something farmer and essayist Wendell Berry and economist John Ikerd have both referred to as the economic colonization of rural America.

"Irreplaceable precious rural resources, including rural people and cultures, are being exploited—not to benefit rural people but to increase the wealth of corporate investors," Ikerd writes.[1] He sees industrial agriculture as a primary means of rural America's colonization: it is extractive and emphasizes profit over long-term health.

On the East Coast, I began to see that extractive mentality clearly for the first time. It often flourishes through ignorance or apathy toward the places that produce our food—an ignorance that can even result in contempt. As Sarah Smarsh writes in her memoir, *Heartland*, "I rarely saw the place I called home described or tended to in political discourse, the news media, or popular culture as anything but a stereotype or something that happened a hundred years ago."[2]

It's easy to exploit places we don't know, places we believe to be unimportant. It's easy to think the soil can last forever if you know nothing of it. But extraction of value at the expense of the land and its people destroys both the "nowheres" and the "somewheres," if you give it time.

Emmett once had an intricate history of dependences and influences that built it from a dry outpost into a bustling, beloved place. But over the years, there has been exploitation, too, which has slowly but steadily depleted the town. One of the first natural resources to be abused here was the soil itself.

Perhaps because of this, of all the memories people have shared with me about Grandpa Dad, stories about his irrigation ditches have become some of my favorites. Irrigation ditch maintenance is important work in this valley, as you might imagine. Farmers need to keep their ditches free of debris and prevent issues such as blockage, seepage, or siltation. Trees, brush, and aquatic weeds can restrict or disrupt water flow, while unkempt embankments give passersby the impression it's a suitable dumping ground for debris and trash.[3] While tree roots can cause flow issues, tree removal can also cause shoreline erosion.

Farmers in this valley generally spray Roundup on their ditch banks to keep vegetation overgrowth at bay and to prevent burrowing animals—such as gophers—from moving in. But Grandpa Dad bought cattle specifically for the purpose of grazing his ditch banks. He used electric fencing to prevent the cattle from trampling on the spots where the irrigation lines cut the bank and then let the cattle regularly "mow" the ditch banks for him. It was surely more expensive and time-consuming than spraying Roundup, and people wondered why he did it. Grandpa Wally told me that he never got a clear answer or explanation as to why Grandpa Dad used this method. He knew his father had the mind of an engineer and liked to work out systems that had great benefits to the land and to his bottom line. Grandpa Dad always called irrigation his hobby, something he delighted in tinkering with and perfecting. The closest Grandpa Dad ever got to explaining his ditch maintenance methodology was, "It makes the land pretty and the animals happy."

And it was pretty. Farmers have told me how much they admired the edges of Grandpa Dad's property. They were pretty and green as a lawn, they told me, always in immaculate condition.

But I knew Grandpa Wally was right: Grandpa Dad surely had other reasons for fostering this system. He'd always been ahead of his time in farming practices. Long before surge irrigation had popular appeal or computer systems to make it work, Grandpa Dad went out to his fields multiple times a day and manually switched the irrigation lines so that they would apply water intermittently in zones over the expanse of his crops. Most farmers wouldn't bother, but Grandpa Dad must've seen the benefits: the prevention of water runoff, the benefits to the soil.

A man like that wouldn't use "ditch bank calves," as he called them, for no reason. So I emailed farmer and author Joel Salatin, a cattle-grazing expert, and asked him whether he thought there were good scientific reasons to implement such a methodology.

"The difference between the two maintenance systems is that one kills and one stimulates," Salatin explained. "If you have a heavy vegetation base, stimulated by strategic pruning (grazing), it will certainly hold the soil in place better than a rootless, naked soil system."

If Grandpa Dad managed the cattle's grazing that way, then he was sending roots deeper and deeper into the soil of this property—preventing soil runoff, strengthening the soil surrounding his ditches, and keeping weeds and pests at bay. According to Salatin, the very saliva of the cattle could stimulate plant growth and feed microbial life in and around the plant.

"There's ample science to substantiate the validity of your great-grandpa's protocols," Salatin said at the end of his email. "He was a wise and smart man."

Grandpa Dad was indeed wise, but even more than that, he was invested. Perhaps he could have saved time, energy, and money by using pesticides, but as a sticker, he knew it was important to care for the land's health. He knew that the beauty of the land and happiness of his animals were, in fact, integral to the flourishing of his place.

Sadly, this isn't a lesson Americans tend to learn, as history shows.

Grazing=strategic pruning

At the United States' founding, over 90 percent of the country's inhabitants lived directly on and from the farm. Ronald Jager wrote in his book *The Fate of Family Farming* that New England farmers often knew their land intimately:

> Knew its quirks, its strengths and weak spots; and to a very large extent it was the produce of that land that was brought to his own table. And he knew his neighbors, and worked with them, and in harvesttime exchanged work with them, each lending a hand to the other. Community, farm, ecosystem, crops, woodlot, animals, family, garden, work, neighbors, worship, leisure—together they promised and, when effective, shaped a coherent system, a total community of life.[4]

But for many Americans, this was not enough. French aristocrat and political scientist Alexis de Tocqueville observed in his classic 1832 work, *Democracy in America*, that the democratic man tends to industrialize his professions—including agriculture—because "however opulent one supposes him, [he] is almost always discontented with his fortune."[5] Because of the expansive, limitless vision of success America seemed to offer, he believed its citizens were drawn toward the possibility of ever greater wealth—and therefore, "they naturally turn their eyes toward commerce and industry, which appear to them the promptest and most powerful means of getting it."[6]

Agricultural operations can grow in a sustainable way that avoids the worst forms of exploitation. But as Tocqueville noted, many Americans who were making "a commerce of agriculture" were cultivating the earth not with longevity in mind but, rather, "with the goal of making it produce in a few years whatever will enrich them."[7] Once the soil was depleted, they would abandon the land and move on. Farmers could be boomers too, Tocqueville seemed to say.

He was right, of course. Farmers can abuse the land and its inhabitants, exploiting the natural resources and peoples surrounding them. Slavery in the South was predicated on just such a demeanor. Many other forms of industrialized agriculture have continued this legacy, subjugating workers, animals, soil, and water to their desire for profit or ease.

Health—of the ground and its produce, as well as of the animals and humans who rely upon it for survival—requires something more, however. Wendell Berry once argued for *Orion Magazine* that "the way we farm affects the local community, and that the economy of the local community affects the way we farm; that the way we farm affects the health and integrity of the local ecosystem, and that the farm is intricately dependent, even economically, upon the health of the local ecosystem." Farms do not exist in "a specialist capsule or a professionalist department" but, rather, "in a webwork of dependences and influences probably more intricate than we will ever understand."[8]

Unfortunately, political and economic leaders in the United States have rarely (if ever) prized this intricate webwork. Instead, they have done their fair share to destroy the health of these local ecosystems, of soil and land and all the creatures and people who rely on it. Emmett is no exception.

In 1909, the U.S. Bureau of Soils declared: "The soil is the one indestructible, immutable asset that the nation possesses. It is the one resource that cannot be exhausted; that cannot be used up."[9]

This statement came as part of a campaign to move Americans west. Farmers and ranchers were originally uncertain how much they could accomplish on farms of the Great Plains and inner West, since these regions were far more arid than the eastern United States—often getting less than twenty inches of rain per year. But agents from the U.S. Department of Agriculture (USDA) claimed in the nineteenth century that "through the miracle of dry farming a fellow could turn [the Plains] to gold."[10] Government agents, railroad companies, and even scientists began peddling the theory that settlement of the West could, in fact, change the climate: that rain would "follow the plow."

Soldier, geologist, and explorer John Wesley Powell condemned all such views as "unscientific and dangerous."[11] But he was a lone voice, fighting against the collective enthusiasm of a western land boom. The Homestead Acts urged millions of hopeful farmers onto prairie lands and river valleys, where they began tearing up native grasses, trees, and brush. Most used a combination of deep plowing, summer fallowing, and growing winter wheat in order to cultivate a profit.

Farmers often referred to the work of irrigation and agriculture as "conquest," Mark Fiege writes in his book *Irrigated Eden*. "They had to defeat nature . . . and make it do their bidding."[12]

This form of conquest in the West—like others—did not often consider the possibility of a bust: of overuse and depletion. But even in these early years, John Wesley Powell suggested that westerners would need something different than conquest to farm in semiarid and arid land. In 1878, Powell published a "Report on the Lands of the Arid Regions of the United States," suggesting that, rather than encouraging homesteaders to spread out in privately owned patchworks across the land, the government ought to encourage farmers to settle in cooperative communities—akin to the Mormon settlements he had observed in Utah. Powell knew that individual initiative, labor, and money would not be sufficient to establish viable irrigation systems. Either private capital would develop (and monopolize) the water, the government would develop and distribute water, or "the people themselves, by co-operative effort such as that of the Mormons, could organize and develop in unison what was impossible for anyone singly."[13]

Powell saw this last option as the most beneficial. He believed that farmers could succeed in the West—but only if they acknowledged the limits of their arid landscape and worked with their neighbors to establish just and equitable irrigation systems. Flourishing farms would be contingent on healthy local communities.

Emmett's early irrigation efforts involved this sort of collaborative energy and collective accountability. Acquiring irrigation required men to associate, to procure public funding, and to work together to determine water rights, best practices, and a way to maintain what they created. It was indeed something they held in common and had to care for as a collective. In 1909,

collaborative energy + collective accountability

the Canyon Canal Water Users Association decided it was time to organize an irrigation district—one that, once the irrigation system was completed, would unite the north and south sides of the valley and cultivate a "united membership of all the landowners ... who would take water from the canal under one irrigation district."[14] The Emmett Irrigation District still exists today and has helped provide water to the valley's farmers for 109 years. Eventually, the valley's farmers would also turn to the Bureau of Reclamation for help building a large dam north of the valley. The Black Canyon Reservoir was constructed as a result, with funds from the Reclamation Extension Act in 1914.[15]

Struggles in years to come would test Emmett farmers' collective energy and reveal the imperfections in their irrigation efforts. Learning to apply the proper amount of water, dealing with issues of water seepage and siltation, combating weeds spread through the water supply, and making sure the land was properly graded—these were just a few of the unforeseen dilemmas farmers would encounter throughout the irrigation process. But the valley's farmers had still achieved enough success to get their farms up and running, and to connect each farm to its neighbor via the water and its requirements.

After World War I started, the price of wheat doubled.[16] High wartime commodity prices convinced farmers to purchase more land, buy more machinery, and improve their yields—even if it required them to go into debt, or to ignore conservation practices, in order to do so. Government leaders, meanwhile, urged agriculturists throughout the United States to grow as much wheat as they could, to feed a world decimated by war. In two years, production of wheat jumped 70 percent: from 45 million acres of wheat in 1917 to 75 million in 1919.[17] Farmers often felt they had to push the land to its limits in order to avoid losing it to the bank. So every year, native grasses across the prairie were "pulverized" and replaced with continuous wheat production (a practice known as monocropping). Traditional conservation practices were abandoned in the name of profit, and a swelling number of acres were put to work by new machines, such as tractors, that could turn wheat into cash. Fields were closely planted to foster high yields and then plowed under right after harvest, which left the soil bare for months before the next planting season.

"This was something audacious," Timothy Egan writes in his book *The Worst Hard Time: The Untold Story of Those Who Survived the Great American Dust Bowl*. "People had been farming since biblical times, and never had any nation set out to produce so much grain on ground that suggested otherwise. If the farmers of the High Plains were laying the foundation for a time bomb that would shatter the natural world, any voices that implied such a thing were muted."[18]

In Idaho, land clearing and overgrazing also left soil exposed and rootless throughout many regions of the state. As ever more cattle and sheep (including Andy Little's massive sheep operation) became dependent on the land, severe riverbank degradation and siltation plagued Idaho's rivers and streams, while intensity of use led to compaction of the soil and depletion of pasture forage throughout its mountains and hillsides. Fights broke out between cattle and sheepherding operations as they battled for available water and pasture.[19]

Eventually, drought would hit both the Midwest and the Northwest. The Plains' naked topsoil would be carried off by strong winds, creating "black blizzards" that blocked out the sun. A 1934 soil erosion study in Idaho, meanwhile, would reveal that more than 27 million acres of land (roughly half the state) had serious soil erosion problems.[20] The "immutable asset" would, in fact, be lost.

Beyond market and governmental pressures, new machinery also convinced many farmers to push their land to the limit in the twentieth century. In the early 1900s, innovative pieces of machinery—such as Henry Ford's small, lightweight tractor, which sold for $750—drastically changed farming customs.[21] Farmers all felt an increasing pressure to specialize, and small-scale farmers often found it difficult to compete with their larger counterparts. Of course, new machinery *could* work with the older, more intricate rhythms of the farm; but profit was maximized through homogenization, not through diversification, and the voices of the age told farmers that success would come through daring, not modesty.

"Higher agricultural prices encouraged farm men and women to specialize their production and participate in the market economy," R. Douglas Hurt writes in his book *Problems of Plenty*. "By so doing, however, they grew more dependent on others."[22] To be clear, traditional farms were often dependent on others in many ways: they were communal and regional and thus encouraged farmers to rely on their neighbors and local agribusinesses.

But this was a new sort of dependence: whereas individual farmers once produced goods that could feed their family, nourish their land, and keep costs down, farmers' debt more than doubled from 1900 to 1920: from $3.2 billion to $8.4 billion.[23] Farmers owed money to commercial, savings, and federal land banks, as well as to mortgage and insurance companies and other lenders—often at interest rates as high as 12 percent.[24] Whereas in 1900, the average farm family produced 60 percent of its food needs, it produced only 40 percent in 1920. "By the end of the Progressive Era," Hurt writes, "most farmers bought most of their food at local grocery stores, and the farm population continued to decline, falling to 30 percent of the national population."[25]

More than fifty thousand farmers suffered bankruptcy in the 1920s (more farm bankruptcies than during the Great Depression) because they had overinvested in land and equipment during the war and raised more wheat, corn, rice, and tobacco than the market demanded.[26] After the Dust Bowl decimated both the health and the hope of Midwestern farming communities, many sought help from the federal government in its wake. The self-sufficiency and diversity that once offered them a safety net had been lost, and so they were desperate for outside assistance.

President Franklin Delano Roosevelt's New Deal promised to help farmers in response—but it did not help all farmers equally. Throughout the 1930s, the U.S. Department of Agriculture focused on aiding "successful" farmers: farmers with "the capital, land, and technology to make the best use of government aid to survive hard times and eventually prosper," as Hurt puts it. "Sharecroppers, tenants, and low-income farmers were essentially ignored by these institutions and organizations because many agricultural officials and leaders considered them too poor, inefficient, and small-scale to improve their farming operations, even with federal support. . . . The Bureau of Agricultural Economics continued to believe that too many farm men and women remained on the land and contributed to overproduction and low prices."[27]

Ironically, however, fewer farmers did not result in less production. Even as government policy encouraged a reduction of agricultural producers, the government's "successful" farmers bought equipment that allowed them to cover more ground with less labor, thus enabling them to buy more land and plant more crops. In the southern United States, tactics aimed at combating overproduction had far-reaching costs, as Jonathan Coppess writes in his history of the Farm Bill: "By 1974 the number of black-operated farms in the South had fallen 95 percent compared to 1920. The misleadingly benign 'surplus labor' and resulting 'efficient reshaping of farm resources' in the South had pronounced and profound human consequences, compounded by racism, segregation, and the fights over civil rights."[28]

Thanks to the efforts of soil scientist Hugh Hammond Bennett, there were some efforts during this time to reinstate conservation practices that had been lost or abandoned during World War I.[29] But we did not recover the biodiversity we had lost. Farms in the West continued to consolidate and specialize—in large part because of both government and market incentives. During World War II and after, international trade took precedent over the cultivation of local markets and sales. Farming was no longer

diversification should be practice
In farming
Just like in stocks   GRACE OLMSTEAD

to be understood as a primarily regional enterprise, meant to feed one's neighbors, but rather as a global (and heavily political) enterprise, meant to foster trade relations and sales overseas. Price supports went to farmers who grew commodities that could be marketed on an international scale—not to farmers growing a diverse array of goods for themselves and for their communities. Thus, farmers grew an increasingly homogenous variety of goods: they focused their production on commodities that could receive federal price supports and could be stored in case of low prices and surplus. Low prices did not encourage farmers to switch to growing a larger diversity of crops or to grow for a more local or regional market: instead, farmers used volume to make up for low prices, assured that the government would back them in case of catastrophic loss or market deficiencies. Farmers worked less with their neighbors and grew increasingly reliant on the federal government and on new technological innovations. They came to see themselves less as part of a local community and more as part of a national and international effort to "feed the world."

"The extension of industrial technology, the growth of urban markets, the increase of transportation facilities, the general rise in the standard of living—all these and related things have exerted tremendous pressure upon the farmer to become a cog in a vast and infinitely complex economic machine," Paul Johnstone wrote in the USDA's 1940 *Yearbook of Agriculture*.[30]

The ideal farm of the modern era was seen as a machine or even a factory: an endeavor of cold efficiency and productivity, not a work of complexity or of culture. Meanwhile, the rest of the

ideal farm

country, and even the world, was still interested in extracting as much out of U.S. farmland as possible.

In the 1970s, U.S. agriculture "became 'more closely integrated with the world economy,' and prices were more dependent upon it," Coppess writes. "Exports fueled stronger prices and powered a sharp ascent up the commodity roller coaster."[31] Trade with China and the Soviet Union opened up a few years later, and a worldwide food shortage caused grain prices to skyrocket. In his book on family farming, economic researcher Marty Strange notes that agricultural exports increased in value from $8 billion to more than $44 billion between 1972 and 1981.[32] In response to this staggering growth, USDA secretary Earl Butz told farmers to "get big or get out"—and in response to his urgings, farmers took out loans and added hundreds of additional acres to their farms.

"Borrowing has had a bad name among conservative farmers for a long time," explains Strange, "and the fear of not being able to pay back a loan has made many reluctant to borrow. But the experts said such attitudes could not be afforded. Farming was no longer a way of life, but a business."[33]

As interest rates were low and inflation was raging, a land boom ensued, with both farmers and high-income nonfarmers rushing to procure acreage. Land prices rose so fast from 1973 to 1981, the annual increase in farmland value was higher (even after inflation adjustments) than net farm income nearly every year. Farmers began spraying with more pesticides, using more fertilizers, and buying new farm machinery—anything to expand their output.

"It's surprising how little the leaders of the 1970s remembered or cared about the nation's worst environmental and social disaster, the Dust Bowl," Stephanie Anderson writes in her book *One Size Fits None*. "After all, it was only forty years in the rearview mirror. . . . Yet [Butz's] concept of 'full production' shifted agriculture back to Dust Bowl–era thinking."[34]

By 1977, U.S. farm production was greatly outstripping foreign demand. From 1973 to 1982, corn storage increased from 484 to 3,120 million bushels.[35] Export prices for wheat, corn, and cotton were falling, creating cash-flow problems for farmers. Export growth slowed to a standstill, influenced by an embargo of grain sales to the Soviet Union, the dwindling of OPEC's influence due to a drop in oil prices, and the growth of agricultural exports in other countries like Brazil and China.

Farmers began defaulting on the loans they had procured for land they could not afford. "By 1984, ordinarily conservative experts were cautiously estimating that between 40 and 50 percent of our commercial-sized family farms had so much debt that they could not remain solvent for long with current interest rates and commodity prices," Strange notes.[36] Many drove their tractors in a giant "tractorcade" to Washington, DC, and protested on the National Mall. Tens of thousands of farms went under.

Grandpa Dad, for his part, refused to get big and refused to get out. He wouldn't take government subsidies (he believed government handouts could lead to recklessness and mismanagement), and he was wary of debt and unnecessary expenses. He never ended up owning more than 120 acres, though he rented 160 additional acres for some years. He once told a newspaper reporter that he "never wanted to be so big he couldn't do his

loss of community church
has decreased
communal connection

own irrigating and control things." His philosophies kept his farm small in a time of exponential growth.

But Emmett experienced the booms and busts of the 1970s and '80s along with everybody else. Many who had started farming or had expanded their operations in the seventies went bankrupt a decade later. At least two of Grandpa Dad's neighbors on the bench lost their farms during this time. One was a young farmer, just starting out, who had invested big in the land and export boom. When corn prices fell, he stored his corn, hoping that prices would increase in coming months. Instead, they dropped almost another twenty dollars a ton, a local farmer told me. As farms grew bigger and more reliant on the government, their owners lost the communal connection that once sustained them through hard times.

Farmers who invested their life's work into the land boom were not the only victims of the bust. New or would-be beginner farmers suffered via the staggering increase in land costs, which dashed their hopes for building a viable farm operation. They couldn't possibly pay for the land by farming it. Many of Emmett's young people were cut off from their roots, lost the "webwork" that might have supported them, and began to drift away.

Roots absorb water and nutrients from the soil. They anchor and support the plants we see aboveground. But roots also are essential to the well-being of the soil itself—part of an intricate, living system we often ignore, because it's down beneath our feet.

Good soil is teeming with life: it is home to a multitude of living organisms both large and small, such as bacteria, protozoa, worms, mites, insects, millipedes, centipedes, spiders, slugs, and snails. In healthy soil, there are more organisms underneath the ground than above it. Most of these life-forms live on plant roots and decaying matter: if there is no humus (decaying organic matter) in the soil, then these microorganisms will struggle.

The symbiotic relationship between roots and fungi is called mycorrhizae: "Mycorrhizal fungi live in and extend from root tissue, bringing nutrients and water to the host plant, suppressing weed growth near it, binding the nearby soil into aggregates that hold water, and probably dozens of other activities we don't understand," Anderson writes in *One Size Fits None*. "Soil is one of the most complex substances on earth, if not the most complex. Humans understand only a tiny fraction of what's actually going on underground, but we do know that billions of microorganisms work together to make soil a living substance."[37]

The area surrounding a plant's roots is known as the rhizosphere, and in this zone, the plant makes compounds that serve as "a veritable cocktail or 'buffet' of resources for anything in the rhizosphere," according to University of Aberdeen researcher Paul Hallett.[38] Roots, exudates, and microorganisms hold the soil together: they serve as indispensable building blocks in our earth. Soil aggregates—both macro- and micro-aggregates—form "microbial villages" that share nutrients, store carbon, and lend health and vigor to the land we observe aboveground.[39] Every time we tear roots out of the soil, we threaten the networks that provide structure and life to this plot of earth. We don't just affect the past or present life of the soil—we harm its future as well. Healthy roots need healthy soil in order to flourish, but healthy soil is also dependent on the roots that have existed in it throughout generations past and present.

This is the wondrous, mysterious life of soil that farmers in centuries past did not understand, when they tore out grasses and sagebrush and plowed up the earth. We are only beginning to understand the degree to which our health is tied to that of our soil—to the communities of microbes that bring wholeness and health to our food, and therefore to us. It's a reality we are increasingly cognizant of and seeking to understand better.

At a meeting of the Idaho Environmental Forum some years ago, state agronomist Marlon Winger declared that the battle for agricultural survival must start "up there on the naked soil": the soil depleted and abandoned.[40] Instability has long been part and parcel of life in this landscape, and it has resulted in an eroded landscape: a land decimated by rootlessness, left bare of fruit and life. No-till farming and the use of "cover crops"—providing the soil with constant ground cover and root protection by planting diverse, soil-replenishing crops on off-years—are efforts aimed at combating this depletion. But many farmers and conservationists worry that no-till farming is not enough: Wes Jackson, cofounder of the Land Institute, has warned that no-till farming still requires herbicide usage and perpetuates the growth of annuals over perennials.[41] Jackson applauds the sustainable agriculture movement and its emphasis on the local production and consumption of fruits and vegetables, but he believes that a truly regenerative system needs to include our cereal production: the rice, wheat, and corn from which the world gets 70 percent of its calories (and which occupies about the same percentage of farm acreage).

"Soon people will realize that annuals are poor managers of nutrients and water, and that agriculture will need to turn to perennials to better manage those resources," Jackson told *The Sun* in a 2010 interview.[42]

Jackson and his companions at the Land Institute are seeking to fix these ills by developing perennial hybrid grains called polycultures, which result from crossing annual grains with their wild perennial relatives. These perennial crops would grow back season after season without farmers ever having to till or plow the soil—thus resulting in deep-rooted, soil-nourishing crops. Jackson calls this a "natural-systems agriculture" and hopes it might replace our current system, which invests only 20 percent of acreage in the growth of perennials.[43] But much depends on the powerful voices of our age and whether people decide to listen this time around: to preserve life in the soil, rather than tearing it up by the roots.

Butz's argument to "get big or get out," adapt or die, has not been reversed in our time. Indeed, in Washington, DC, and elsewhere, it seems to be as popular as ever. In October 2019, USDA secretary Sonny Perdue shared Butz's mantra with a roomful of farmers in Wisconsin, a state that lost nearly two dairy farmers a day that year due to a massive downturn in milk prices.[44] As John

[handwritten margin note:] we shouldn't be able to get any fruit or veggie @ any time of the year

Ikerd has noted, as we've built up fewer, larger, and more special-ized farms, and decreased both local markets and locally pur-chased inputs, "many rural communities seem to have lost their purpose."[45] Small farm towns are increasingly seen as "middle of nowheres," practically nonexistent in the eyes of the larger world.

We've undervalued the degree to which those small, con-nected farms mattered: how the bonds of life they cultivated in their lifetime were thick and nourishing, how the virtues they fostered mattered for communal health. Small farmers built a culture in Emmett—a shared set of beliefs, values, goals, and practices—that emphasized stewardship, neighborliness, volun-tarism, and responsibility. The farmers that undergirded this community worked hard to build up job opportunities for the kids who grew up there, and did their best to keep health in the soil.

These days, however, highly educated Americans cluster in "winner-take-all cities" such as Los Angeles, New York City, or Chicago, and "Americans with less education are often either left behind in stagnant economies or pushed out of expensive, dy-namic cities."[46]

It is not difficult to see how dangerous this situation could be for our rural communities. Places that used to be healthy have grown frail. Many rural communities are increasingly empty of people and of hope. But for some reason, instead of seeing an outpouring of alarm or concern over these developments, advo-cates for rural America have met with a growing amount of pushback and disdain. Maria Kefalas told me in a phone inter-view that she remembers her publisher asking her, as she was cowriting her book *Hollowing Out the Middle*, "So what if rural

America dies?" Nobody she knew cared about "flyover country," the rural stretches of America where little exciting or meaningful activity seemed to happen.

In an interview with Robert Wuthnow, author of *The Left Behind: Decline and Rage in Rural America*, *Vox* reporter Sean Illing suggested that rural America is not a place where people have been left behind, but rather a place where people have "chosen not to keep up."[47] Any difficulties countryfolk were experiencing in our time, he seemed to suggest, were their own fault.

Illing's suggestion that rural people have "chosen not to keep up" fits perfectly with the transitory language of success in our culture: the fact that mobility is equated with success, and rootedness with failure. But he's wrong, too, because Emmett's farmers and townspeople *have* tried to keep up over time: there have always been efforts to follow the latest fad, to embrace the latest boom, or to listen to the advice of the current agricultural experts. Some of these efforts may have had a good impact on the town. But a lot of them ended in busts, depletion, and bankruptcy. Emmett has suffered not because it didn't keep up—but because it did.

Farm towns have now experienced countless cycles of conquest and depletion, boom and bust. Timber and riverbed, flora and fauna have experienced patterns of overuse and exhaustion. The constant waves of exodus bleed nourishment from the soil, eroding the ground they leave behind.

Sir Albert Howard, a turn-of-the-century botanist who studied sustainable agriculture in India, suggested that soil regenerates through a life cycle of death, decay, and regrowth. To cultivate health, we must be investing as much (or more) fertility in the earth as we take from it.[48] If we instead deplete the ground's resources, future generations pay the price. I fear that as those of us who grew up in the soil of our small farm towns leave, we remove the material that should have remained, that would have resulted in hope and nourishment for the next generation.

The good news is that, despite the damage caused by boomers, there is hope, thanks to the stickers who have stayed and who give back to the soil, both literally and metaphorically.

Chapter Five

A group of Brown Swiss cattle stand together in a sprawling pasture, feasting on grass. It's easy, from a distance, to see this field as a monotonous green mass—but look closer, and you begin to see a diverse tapestry. The cattle eat red and white clover (which are technically legumes) alongside forage grasses like wild rye, orchard grass, bluegrass, and fescue—to name just a few. Most pastures also contain a diverse array of herbs like dandelion, yarrow, and plantain. The cattle bear an ear tag with a number and letter for identification, along with an affectionate name printed below (such as Paxton or Kid). The sound of their satisfied munching and crunching fills the air, while swallows dance overhead in a dizzying profusion, swooping down to eat bugs that the cattle disturb in the pasture.

All these tall grasses have correspondingly deep roots in this soil. After the cattle graze this grass—usually down to about four inches from the ground—they will head for a new section of pasture. Behind them, they leave nitrogen-rich urine and manure to fertilize the soil. Meanwhile, plant roots "die back" to the degree their vegetation has been pruned aboveground, leaving organic matter—carbon—stored within the soil. This paddock will then rest until the grass grows high again and the roots have penetrated even deeper into the earth. As Ben Falk writes in *The Resilient Farm and Homestead*, "You only build soil as deeply as you can get plant roots to penetrate (what comes up must go down), so the taller you let your yard or pasture grow before it's cut or grazed, the more soil you're making (and CO_2 you're sequestering)."[1]

If Grandpa Dad's "ditch bank calves" defied convention in order to encourage rootedness on a small scale, these cattle are a symbol of full-scale agricultural revolt. They are engaged in a process known as regenerative grazing: one that grows soil and encourages rootedness, rather than depletes or destroys the land. In response to the extraction and depletion of modern farming practices, farms like this one have set themselves up to resist. They are helping bring about the future Wes Jackson has dreamed of: one in which perennial roots offer health and wholeness to depleted farmland.

Saint John's Organic Farm is a pasture-based, small-scale beef farm between Emmett's town limits and the southern slope, and they have worked for decades to restore soil decimated by exploitative methods. I discovered this 160-acre family farm via Facebook while researching agriculture in Emmett and was immediately fascinated by their farming model. I had interviewed a few farmers like this out in Virginia but had not yet encountered many in my own farm community back in Idaho. In a decidedly Republican state and county, Saint John's Organic Farm touted a pro-environmentalist, stewardship-minded ethic on their website, assuring customers that "we use less fossil fuel, have less water runoff, and run into fewer pest problems than our industrial counterparts." What's more, the owners, the Dills, tie their farming methodology back to their Christian beliefs:

Being thankful to God for the earth, His good creation, we seek to live in ways that protect and nurture the earth while enjoying its beauty and bounty. This means we purpose to farm in ways that are sound agriculturally, environmentally, financially, and emotionally. We rely on farming practices old and new: attending to water, air and soil quality, paying our workers a decent wage, keeping our farm in good order, working together with family and friends. . . . As providers for people and as caretakers of the earth, we seek what is best for you and the world we inhabit, and to offer a vision of sustainable agriculture for future generations.[2]

After reading this, I was determined to interview the Dills. But over the course of a month and a half, they did not return my phone calls or emails.

At first, I felt like giving up. But then I interviewed the Tyler family, who own an orchard on Emmett's south slopes. We talked about the difficulties of procuring orchard workers, federal crop insurance, and the town's roots as a farming community. I asked Mr. Tyler, who is also the town pharmacist, if he knew of many local organic productions in the area.

He immediately asked if I had seen Saint John's Farm. "They've really had to fight local government over chemical spraying," he said. "They have signs all over their property saying that it's a spray-free zone."

Indiscriminate spraying—by airplane and by truck—is a common thing in Idaho, although it's become increasingly controversial. In the summers, many counties spray for mosquitoes without offering so much as a notice to local residents. I could see why such an environment could make organic farming next to impossible.

"Saint John's has the prettiest land you'll see anywhere," Tyler said. He added that although he wasn't sure what exactly the Dills were doing to accomplish this, it was obviously working.

That clinched it for me. I had to talk to these people—to find out more about their farming methodology and vision for agriculture, as well as their hopes for Emmett itself.

⚜

It is a quiet October afternoon. The air feels cool and fresh as I walk up to the Dills' porch, slightly in awe of my own brazenness. I stand unannounced and uninvited at their front door. I knock a couple of times and wait. I hear footsteps, and a middle-aged man opens the door. He wears a frank—albeit curious—smile.

"Hi," I say apologetically. "I'm Gracy Olmstead, the writer who won't leave you alone."

The man laughs, introduces himself as Peter Dill, and welcomes me in. He says he is impressed by my persistence and explains that the family has been rather busy of late.

I sit across from Peter in a wooden rocking chair. The family's living room is warm and comfortable, with a wood-burning stove in one corner and a vibrant green carpet, circa 1970, adorning the floor. The room's shelves are stuffed with books, and I can see a large piano and a harp tucked around the corner.

Peter Dill folds his hands. "If it's all right, I would like to ask you some questions," he says.

I nod. This is not unexpected for me: I know many people are suspicious of journalists. And often, when or if a farmer is doing something decidedly different from the norm in his community or state, there's an even greater proclivity toward hesitancy. Who knows if this is how Peter Dill feels. But I have come prepared to explain myself.

As I talk about my grandfathers and their legacy, Peter nods. He asks me why I moved to Washington, DC, so I tell him about college, and how I started reading the work of Wendell Berry. When I mention Berry's name, his eyes light up. This evidently strikes a chord.

Near the end of our conversation, a slight woman with long, dark hair walks in. She smiles at me and extends her hand, introducing herself as Susan Dill, Peter's wife. She asks me if I'd like to stay for lunch. "We mostly have leftovers, but you're welcome to what we have," she says.

I thank them but say I have to leave—and ask if it would be all right if I contact them again in the future. They both nod and smile.

A few months later, I find myself again in the Dills' living room, sitting in the same rocking chair, as Peter and Susan settle on the couch across from me. They are both wearing the exact same shade of turquoise. Susan wears a simple cross necklace. As I take notes, they begin to share their story.

Susan grew up in Emmett: her grandparents moved to the valley and started a farm here in this valley in 1934. Susan remembers her family delivering fresh milk to town inhabitants, once upon a time—back when fresh milk in glass bottles still appeared on your doorstep. Her parents continued the dairy and farm operation, rotating corn and wheat crops along with an occasional alfalfa crop.

Peter, meanwhile, was born and raised in Seattle. He met Susan at the University of Washington, and after they were married, the couple became interested in farming. Their original plan was to start a farm of their own in Washington, but when they visited Susan's family over the holidays one winter, they realized the Emmett farm was in dire trouble. They decided to return home and help save the family farm.

When Peter and Susan returned to Emmett, they had a six-year-old son, a four-year-old daughter, and a son who was born just days after they arrived back in town. They wanted to build a farm counter to convention: a farm focused on both health over profit and quality over quantity. They immediately began to transition the farm to organic.

Peter and Susan wanted to replenish the life of their soil—to make radical changes in order to bring back its health. When they first began converting their land to organic, soil tests showed that conventional fruit-farming methods had given them a soil with traces of arsenic and other harmful chemicals. So they hauled compost onto depleted fields, did soil tests, and brought in micronutrients. Now, after decades of intense care, their land is healthy and whole again.

"We were trying to see through new eyes," Peter says. "It is a process, to think about and practice farming differently." Saint John's employs no-till and management-intensive grazing methodologies: the family moves portable electric fences daily so that their cattle can constantly graze on fresh pasture, thus speeding pasture regrowth, boosting soil health, reducing costs, and mitigating erosion.[3]

The Dills also switched to a surge irrigation system, which conserves water and prevents sediment loss. While these systems are expensive to implement, the ecological and financial savings have made them increasingly popular for farmers. With a surge system, farmers use a flat irrigation pipe and surge valve to apply water intermittently, thus wetting the soil in "zones." When water is reintroduced to a furrow that is already wet, it moves quickly past the wet soil to the next dry patch of ground, without soaking too deep into the soil.[4] According to some studies, surge irrigation can save 20 to 50 percent more water than alternative systems.[5] And that matters in Idaho: farmers here use more water in irrigation than in any other state except California, and many of its irrigation systems could be updated to conserve available water supply.[6]

In 2018, the Dills installed a water line to cut their diesel usage—previously, they had to load a thousand-gallon tank of water on their trailer and drive it out to water their cattle during the winter. Now, the water line provides a fresher, greener alternative. Their diesel usage was already down to about a hundred gallons a year due to the farm's self-sufficient design and the way they do most things by hand. But with the water line, they were able to cut that number in half.

When they first started transitioning their family farm, the Dills sold organic-certified milk and were one of the first dairies in Idaho to do so. It wasn't long before they were fighting the Idaho attorney general for the right to sell raw milk, and for a while, they were the only provider of raw milk in the state. But now, Peter tells me, there are over a hundred raw-milk providers throughout Idaho. After a while, the Dills stopped selling milk and began focusing on selling grass-finished organic beef. "We stopped selling the raw milk, in part, because it was available," Peter explains. "We wanted to simplify."

The Dills' sales may have simplified, but the operation they run is still diverse and multifaceted. They care for pasture-raised chickens, pigs, rabbits, and horses alongside their cattle. They tend an orchard, a berry patch, and a large vegetable garden. They swathe their own hay in the pastures for winter storage—primarily for their pregnant cows, which often need supplemental feed in the winter and early spring. And they strive to provide a safe habitat for barn owls, foxes, and other wild animals that serve as a natural pest control. They are planting trees throughout their property and recently added a pollinator meadow and hedgerow to encourage the health of local bee and butterfly populations. Not only do they encourage the growth of the roots currently embedded in their land, but they are constantly sending more roots down into the soil to join them.

The couple's children, now grown, have worked extensively on the farm: helping birth calves, clean out irrigation ditches, and move cattle, among other chores. They bring their own spark and creativity to the farm: Claire Dill has named newborn calves after beloved storybook characters like Tumnus and Whatsit, and Aaron Dill, the oldest, recently built a sauna on the farm property. Jonathan Dill, the youngest, has delivered and resuscitated twin calves by himself. But the Dill children are still in their early to mid-twenties and figuring out what careers they might like to pursue. Both Peter and Susan have encouraged their children to use their independent years post–high school to travel widely and pursue studies they are passionate about.

That said, all three children seem to have caught their parents' passion for Saint John's and can see and understand the vision behind the family farm. They've grown up reading the work of agricultural visionaries like Wendell Berry and have watched their parents fight to make this land beautiful and whole.

"The farm must be winsome for young people," Peter tells me. "Because if the kids don't want to stay, the future is lost." Susan notes that it is important, for this reason, to have a community of people who support and help out on the farm. Farmers who work in isolation are likely to estrange their children from the farm because of its grueling and lonely labors. The farmers who are surrounded by community, and work with a team of individuals, will foster a vision of life that is wholesome and lively for their children.

In these (and many other) ways, the Dills have given their children an alternative vision of the American Dream—one that draws them to the farm, rather than distancing them from it. Instead of focusing on mobility, endless choice, or the accumulation of things, Peter and Susan believe it is important that their children learn to find joy in creation and beauty.

"If we define the American Dream in terms of mobility, more things, more money, we've been sold a bill of goods," Peter says. He points at a framed embroidery on the living room wall. It depicts a Bible verse from the book of Micah: "What does the Lord require of you but to do justice, and to love kindness, and to walk humbly with your God?"

Peter and Susan look up at it and then turn back toward me.

"Being content, living within a community, caring for people— that sounds like the real dream," Peter says. "It's romantic, and it's reality. It's a way of life worth living. Why settle for money, things, and disconnection?" He pauses. "We will do future generations an enormous favor if we reinvent the American Dream."

[handwritten margin note: Why settle for money, things and disconnection?]

In many ways, Peter and Susan Dill seem to be Grandpa Dad's ideological and spiritual heirs in Emmett: a couple carrying on the values of rootedness, sustainability, and caring that so characterized his life. But in an ecological sense, they've also gone above and beyond what he was able to achieve in his lifetime: suggesting that we can build upon the legacy and knowledge of our forebears, if we stick around and pay attention.

Like many of Grandpa Dad's farming methodologies, Saint John's grass-fed, grass-finished beef operation is not normal. The

Dills move their cattle constantly from one small paddock to another, allowing them a short amount of time to graze down the grass and fertilize the land before moving them to fresh pasture. The cattle graze intensively for a short amount of time, and then the land rests for a long period. Bison on the prairie would have once grazed the Great Plains similarly: wild herding animals generally bunch tightly, travel in groups, and produce high concentrations of manure in a given grazing area. They then "surf" from one patch of grass to another, moving on to avoid predators or feeding on ground they have soiled.[7] The bison, scientists have suggested, helped create the deep-rooted, lush prairie grasses that farmers ignorantly plowed up before the Dust Bowl.

Conventional grazing, in contrast, follows a far different set of rhythms. Most ranchers put their cattle in large pastures where they graze erratically and at will, eating whatever they like best and leaving the rest untouched. Once the ground is "grazed up" (approximately once every few months), ranchers move the cattle to new pasture. The system works well to cultivate the cattle's health and size. But land where the vegetation is cherry-picked often suffers from a multitude of problems: Livestock eventually overgraze and kill the most nutritious grasses, leading to a proliferation of woody plants and weeds. Manure and urine are unevenly distributed. The root systems we cannot see become heavily depleted—because the grasses don't get that period of long rest and regrowth that cultivates deep-rootedness.

The problems don't end in the conventional pasture, however. Steers raised on most calf-cow operations are grass-fed only until they are weaned. Ranchers then move them to a mini feedlot,

are we humans like grass needing rest/rootedness

where they begin eating corn. In *One Size Fits None*, Stephanie Anderson notes that cattle, which are ruminant animals, are "designed to eat and digest grass. But steers fatten quickly on grain, and America's corn and soybean growers are producing a surplus of both, making these grains relatively cheap."[8] After several months, the steer is sold at auction and ends up at a concentrated animal feeding operation (CAFO), "whose mission is to fatten animals for slaughter 'efficiently' by keeping them in grassless feedlots and feeding them carefully controlled rations—a process called finishing. The larger the CAFO, the thinking goes, the more efficient it is."[9]

CAFOs feed cattle a combination of corn, soybeans, grains, corn silage, and other nonherbivorous material, along with synthetic growth hormones and antibiotics. Because of the size of these operations and the cheapness of their feed, the meat produced is also cheap, thus allowing modern Americans to consume more meat for less money than at any other time in human history. But many have argued that there is a hidden health cost to this meat. The nutritious value of grass-fed, grass-finished beef—like that produced by the Dills—far surpasses that of the conventionally produced beef one might get from Tyson Foods.

Cheap beef isn't just worse for us nutritionally, it also comes at great cost to the land. Conventional grazing replaces a cyclical, root-deepening system with a static, carbon-releasing system— one that is steadily depleting and destroying our soil, water, and grasslands. If regenerative productions were to become more widespread, farms would produce less beef per acre, and the change would require the U.S. population to consume less meat.[10]

This change would be difficult, but farmers like the Dills are doing the hard work of seeking to adapt their productions to protect the soil and preserve it for generations. Surely, we as consumers can make some changes too.

As I drive away from Saint John's, I feel more hope in the future of Emmett, more excited for the future, than I have felt in quite some time. Perhaps we boomers haven't done irreparable damage after all.

But will the Dills be able to continue their work? My enthusiasm for their individual efforts dampens as I consider the bigger picture. The cost of today's agriculture extends far beyond the soil. As agriculture has grown more monolithic and global in its reach, there have been widespread economic consequences. Giant agribusinesses have weakened the communities that sustained my family of farmers, wearing out the stickers and squelching voices of protest.

Chapter Six

It is early May. Trees in Emmett are turning green, the sides of the road are lined with cattails, and magpies occasionally skitter across the road as I drive toward the Emmett bench, where Tracy Walton is planting corn in his fields. I see Tracy waving from his red tractor as he moves through a tilled field, and I pull to the side of the road. He stops and waits for me as I trudge through the dirt. Tracy wears a faded but clean T-shirt, a baseball cap, and sturdy work boots as I walk up to him and shake his hand.

"Can you take notes while we drive?" he asks.

I nod and climb into the red tractor. It has seats for two people, air-conditioning, and a GPS system. Unlike the variable planting rhythms of the past, Tracy's tractor helps him track seeding depth and spacing as he works his way through the field. Straight, evenly spaced rows once depended on the skill and attentiveness of the farmer—but these days, GPS-enabled tractors create arrow-straight lines of seed, all uniformly planted and spaced.

I had spent the past month calling Emmett farmers from my little house in Virginia. Many didn't return my voice- or emails. Those who did often sounded suspicious and unsure. After several failed attempts at scheduling interviews, I began mentioning my grandfather at the outset of every phone call.

"I grew up in Idaho," I'd say. "My grandfather is Wally Howard."

Voices immediately grew warm. "Wally!" several exclaimed, followed quickly by the question, "So how did you end up out there in Virginia?"

Many farmers seemed skeptical that a writer from a big city would be interested in the workings of a small agricultural community. Indeed, the more I talked to these farmers, the more I realized how invisible local farm communities can feel in the face of a concentrating agricultural industry and a clueless, disinterested public. Many are used to keeping their heads down and working tenaciously, no matter how tough things get. But many crop and dairy farmers know firsthand that this powerlessness can eventually result in collapse.

Farmers usually wait to plant corn until the soil temperature is at least fifty degrees; at that point, the corn seed generally takes three to four weeks to germinate. The corn seed will absorb 30 percent of its weight in water, and seven to ten days later, the seed's coleoptile—a protective plant tissue that encloses the emerging shoot—will spring upward from the soil.[1] The inner leaves of the corn stalk will slowly unfold and begin photosynthesizing the sunlight above them. In the fall, the corn will be ripe for harvest.

Idaho farmers grow 70 percent of the hybrid temperate sweet corn seed produced around the world, in addition to seeds for carrots, onions, turnips, lettuces, alfalfa, radishes, clover, sugar beets, and Kentucky bluegrass. Seed farming usually has a slightly different rhythm than other farmers' growing season—lettuce, for instance, will be harvested after it has flowered and its light-gray pappi have emerged. Sweet corn seed won't be harvested until a month or two after it would be harvested for market: farmers wait until the moisture of their corn is approximately 30 to 50 percent, then use specialized harvesting equipment to keep the corn husk intact as protection for the kernels within. After the corn is processed, it is dried for an additional seventy-two hours, then cleaned, sorted, and packed.[2]

Seed cultivation is an ancient practice, one traditionally controlled and led by farmers. They have long worked to develop plants with reliability and durability, plants that can provide sustenance for their communities. The cornucopia of fruits, vegetables, and grains we eat today are the result of this grassroots-driven process.

Nowadays, however, seeds are another realm of agricultural production that has been transformed by monopolization and its resultant emphasis on corporate profit over ecological diversity or local health. Many of today's farmers buy hybrid seeds from agribusinesses who curate specific traits within their seeds: increased yield or disease resistance, for example. Farmers like Tracy have contracts with these seed companies to cultivate their product, which the companies will then sell to other farmers.

In the 1930s, hybrid seeds drastically changed the rhythms of seed preservation and cultivation in the United States. In the 1940s, Dr. W. F. Owens discovered cytoplasmic male sterility in sugar beets, leading to the development of a high-yielding sugar beet hybrid, and the discovery of monogerm seed in 1948 eliminated the need for the hand-thinning once required for open-pollinated multigerm cultivars.[3] When high-yielding hybrid corn entered the market, new seed companies sprung up to sell this corn every year to eager farmers. Over the next few decades, the Green Revolution encouraged farmers at home and abroad to abandon traditional methodologies in favor of new innovations like high-yielding seed varieties, chemical fertilizers, and agrochemicals.[4]

As seed biotechnology developed, large agribusiness companies began buying up smaller firms in order to accumulate more intellectual property rights.[5] While there are still seed banks owned by the government, land grant universities, and small seed companies, the world's largest germplasm library belongs to Monsanto (and therefore to Bayer, which acquired Monsanto in 2018). In order to access that store of germplasm, companies have to license it—but, as Kristina Hubbard writes in her 2009 report "Out of Hand," it is very expensive to license genetics from these firms. At the time her report was published, "at least 200 independent seed companies [had] been lost in the last thirteen years alone."[6]

Tracy farms eight hundred acres along the Emmett bench, just down the road from where Grandpa Dad used to farm. He has grown corn, teff (an Ethiopian grass with seeds that are used for flour), and sugar beet seed for seed companies over the years.

Domesticated sugar beets are considered a biennial, with roots forming the first year and the stalks and seeds forming the second season. Farmers plant stecklings (the name for small, late-planted biennial root crops) the first year, then harvest and overwinter them before replanting the following season for seed production. Farmers will plant the stecklings in male (pollinator) and female strips. The male plants have multigerm flowers with fused seeds, which can create several seedlings upon planting. The female plants, by contrast, produce monogerm flowers with one germ per seed. To ease the backbreaking work of sugar beet thinning, farmers save and use only the female (monogerm) seeds.[7]

As we slowly move through the cornfield, Tracy points to the irrigation ditch next to us and tells me that Grandpa Dad (who he calls Walt) dug it himself. In the corner of the field, he says, there was once a giant tree underneath which Grandpa Dad used to eat his lunch every day. I can hear the fondness and reverence in his voice. Tracy grew up around these "old-timers." As a member of the Gem County Farm Bureau, he has worked to preserve their memories and farm stories—the pieces of local culture they cultivated in their lifetime. The bureau tapes old farmers talking about their lives, walking around their farms, and proffering advice to the next generation. They call these local legends "the Gems" of Gem County.

Farmers here have always been close. In the old days, there were a lot more farms on this bench, and they were smaller operations, usually farming between sixty and one hundred acres. They were the original subsistence farms of the West: focused on self-sufficiency, fostering a diverse swath of animal and plant life.

But now, Tracy guesses, there are likely fewer than six dairies in the area, and they are much larger operations. Crop farmers like himself are less common, and their businesses cover more acreage. Many folks in this river valley, over the past several decades, have gotten big or gotten out.

Tracy grows a very diverse array of crops for the modern farmer: corn, hay, wheat, soybeans, sugar beets, alfalfa, and teff. Much of what Tracy grows depends on the contracts he receives—with other local farmers or with agribusiness companies. Many large commodity crops, such as wheat or corn, can be stored at local grain elevators as farmers wait for the market price to rise. Farmers can then sell their crops to local processors or to grain terminals who will ship the commodity overseas. In the past, Tracy has sold corn to local dairy owners Joe and Lucy Lourenco as well as to large agribusinesses Lansing Trade Group and the J.R. Simplot Company. Idaho is the second-largest U.S. producer of hay and the top-ranking producer of organic-certified hay in the country.

Despite Tracy's years of hard work and farming experience, however, recent growing seasons have been fraught and difficult. Prices are low, yet seed is increasingly expensive as the seed market rapidly consolidates in the hands of a few companies who dominate the industry. "This is the year where you do everything right and hopefully break even," he tells me, a look of grim determination on his face.

Doing business with big seed companies is often difficult for farmers: while the exact verbiage of their licensing contracts is confidential, it has been reported that they contain strict stipulations regarding insect management, chemical use, and sales (if the farmer is growing seed to be used as seed).[8] Farmers no longer own the seed they plant in their fields; the fate of their crop is often highly dependent on the decisions of companies far removed from their local context. Monsanto forbids farmers from saving or sharing their seed and asserts their right to inspect farmers' property upon request. One seed company owner told Hubbard that Monsanto has audited its licensees every year and "knows what you got in the bank and what's in your fields— everything we know, they know."[9] In 2013, *The Guardian* reported that Monsanto had sued hundreds of small farmers in an effort to protect its intellectual property rights.[10]

Tracy admits to me that, even though he tends to be pretty libertarian on most issues, he does feel that the seed industry should receive more oversight. He sees falling commodity prices and surging seed costs as an unfair burden on farmers seeking to "feed the world."

But farmers have little choice these days: four seed companies now dominate the brand-name seed market, accounting for more than 60 percent of global proprietary seed sales. Philip Howard of Michigan State University published seed industry consolidation charts in 2008 and 2013 that depicted the stark acceleration of acquisitions and mergers throughout the seed industry since 1996.[11] His 2018 chart shows that the so-called Big Six—Monsanto, DuPont, Syngenta, Dow, Bayer, and BASF—have become the Big Four: Bayer, BASF, ChemChina, and Corteva. What's more, many of these companies do not just sell seed—they sell the "companion chemical" necessary to grow that seed. As Claire Kelloway explained in an article for *Washington Monthly,* "even as farmers are paying monopoly prices for a diminishing selection of seed strains produced by [a] handful of giant corporations, they also are paying monopoly prices for fertilizers and pesticides, often to the same corporations."[12]

Mergers and acquisitions in the world of agribusiness have transformed more than the worlds of seed and agrochemicals. Today, just four companies control 84 percent of cattle slaughter, 65 percent of pork slaughter, and 53 percent of chicken slaughter, according to *Pacific Standard.*[13] Dean Foods and Smithfield Foods dominate the dairy and pork industries, respectively. And both grocers and brand-name products have been consolidating for the past few decades. Many have decried the "illusion of choice" available to modern consumers, as the thousands of colorful brands lining grocery store shelves belong to a mere handful of companies, such as General Mills or Coca-Cola.[14]

But this lack of agribusiness diversity also hurts farmers: as Kelloway and others at the Open Markets Institute have demonstrated, consolidation of agribusiness often hampers the ability of farmers to make a fair profit.

"In many rural communities, a farmer raising animals for slaughter has the 'choice' of selling to only one slaughterhouse," Austin Frerick, deputy director of the Thurman Arnold Project at Yale, wrote in 2019. "And because Tyson is often the only buyer in town, it calls the shots, dictating everything from the facilities a farmer builds on her farm, to the feed she uses, to the price the farmer receives for full-grown chickens."[15] Industry consolidation affects these farmers' bottom lines, their ability to adopt more sustainable practices, and their ability to fairly pay their employees. But there's also a trickle-down effect this consolidation creates for the local community, Frerick notes: "Because farmers and other rural workers make less money, they also spend less money within their communities, creating a ripple effect that negatively impacts other local businesses. As a result, rural communities are hollowing out. Young people are leaving in droves, and the folks left behind are struggling to make ends meet."

⸙

"No more milking cows," Lucy Lourenco tells me over the phone.

Her voice is resigned, relieved in some ways. Lucy was Grandpa Dad's neighbor and friend, and so I grew up hearing stories about her, particularly about her love for her animals and her dairy. But this decision has been a long time coming.

Lucy and Joe Lourenco emigrated from Portugal in 1984. They were only nineteen and twenty-four years old, respectively, and newly married. Neither could speak English. They spent the first few years of their life in the United States working in California, planning to save up $20,000 and return home to Portugal. But after a few years, they began dreaming about starting a dairy. Idaho seemed like the perfect place to begin such a venture, so they bought property on the Emmett bench in 1992, next door to Grandpa Dad and the Waltons, and have lived and worked there ever since.

Grandpa Dad was the first person to welcome Lucy and Joe to the neighborhood. Lucy remembers him coming up the driveway with a friendly smile, his hands clasped behind his back as he talked to them. Other folks would look at them oddly in days to come, perhaps because of their thick accents, Lucy surmises. But Grandpa Dad was always kind to them, she says. They would invite him over for dinner and make him traditional Portuguese fish soup, and they often shared their homemade chouriço—a sausage made with paprika, garlic, salt, and pepper, and marinated in Portuguese red wine—with Grandpa Dad, Grandpa Wally, and my father, Rick.

Grandpa Dad loved having Joe and Lucy next door. He was proud of their resolve and work ethic. The old, wizened farmer became friends with the young Portuguese couple who taught themselves how to farm, how to speak, read, and write in English.

"He was a motivated person and hardworking," Lucy tells me. "He was not one of those people with fancy equipment; he didn't make us feel like we had nothing but junk." The first tractor Lucy and Joe bought was a tiny antique and cost them $500. They often had to make do with less, or with older equipment, while money was tight. But I have a picture of Grandpa Dad in his twenties, sitting atop a broken-down tractor and plow that he'd jerry-rigged to attach to a team of horses. He knew what it felt like to make do with less, to build prosperity out of someone else's junk.

Now in her fifties, Lucy's black hair is streaked with a bit of gray, but she is as feisty and determined as ever. You can still see in her the nineteen-year-old bride who was determined to start a new life in a new country. On her kitchen wall is a framed calendar page from February 1993, which she refers to as "the month that almost killed our dream." The Lourencos had just settled in the valley and started their dairy. But the day before a truck was supposed to pick up their first milk delivery, a snowstorm blasted through the valley, burying their long driveway in snow. Lucy and Joe did not have any snow-shoveling equipment, so they chipped away at the deluge with shovels, making little to no headway. The snow continued to bury their farm, threatening to bury their fledgling dairy with it. Thankfully, it rained just in time. The snow melted away, the truck was able to pick up their milk delivery, and they were saved.

Lucy saw it as a good omen for the future—God's blessing on their enterprise—so she tore out the calendar page and saved it. "We started with forty cows and barely made enough money to eat," Lucy says. "But it's a beautiful business."

Lucy and Joe typify the incredible grit and resiliency that immigrants to this and other regions of the United States have demonstrated throughout the centuries. They also have experienced, however, the loneliness and difficulty associated with agricultural entrepreneurship. In 2019, Lucy and Joe decided to sell their dairy. They were ready for a less stressful career path. They got rid of all their milking cows except twenty, which they used to feed some of their young stock. They then sold their remaining cattle—steers, heifers, and bulls—the following year. They now plan to continue crop farming their six hundred acres, growing corn, grain, and hay. Joe has always preferred crop farming to dairying anyway.

"Everybody thinks we sold because we're broke," Lucy says. "But we were just tired." Lucy handles all the bookkeeping and finances. She's always kept the accounting in order and makes sure they have money saved for the bad years. Selling the dairy enabled them to pay everything they owed, and now they feel like they have a clean slate. The dairy may not have reaped the harvest Lucy and Joe expected when they first started farming here almost thirty years ago, but it is helping them enter a new season—one in which they hope to be less stressed and more self-sufficient.

Dairying is an increasingly challenging enterprise for farmers throughout the United States. Dairy is Idaho's top agricultural industry: its exports bring in approximately $320 million per year.[16] But in recent years, overproduction has taken a toll on dairy's profits all throughout the United States.

Although milk prices have historically not remained at low or break-even levels for more than a year, milk has now sold under break-even prices for multiple years, according to University of Idaho Extension agricultural economist Ben Eborn. This trend has prompted farmers to dump millions of gallons of excess milk in fields, manure lagoons, or animal feed.[17] Between 2000 and 2018, the United States lost half of its dairy farmers, and more are going out of business every year.[18] The state of Wisconsin lost seven hundred dairies in 2018 alone.[19]

The dairies that are going out of business are primarily small. In Vermont, which has lost nearly one-third of its dairies over the past decade, the vast majority that have closed down had fewer than two hundred cows. But even while these small operations disappear, the number of Vermont dairies with seven hundred or more cows has doubled in the last five years, according to the state's Agency of Agriculture, Food, and Markets.[20]

Dairy farming here in Idaho used to be a local industry. My grandpa Wally remembers driving a dairy truck when he was in high school, helping deliver fresh milk to Emmett's townspeople. Susan Dill's grandfather was one of several dairy owners in and around Emmett. In the 1960s, one Meridian, Idaho, farmer recalled, there were eight dairies on his square mile. "Only people my age remember the beautiful valley and the small, well-kept farms," he told the *Press-Tribune*.[21]

These days, the state has fewer dairies than ever before—approximately five hundred in all—but production is as high as it has ever been.[22] Rather than servicing a local clientele, today's dairies supply large food producers and manufacturers like J.R. Simplot, Idaho Milk Products, Glanbia Foods, and Chobani. The average Idaho dairy cow produces 58 percent more milk today than it did in 1980, according to *Idaho Statesman* reporter Zach Kyle; and in order to meet its food needs, Idaho's crop farmers are producing more field corn and alfalfa than ever before.[23] Dairy feedlots have proliferated throughout the Magic Valley region of the state, producing the equivalent in raw sewage of 17 million people.[24] Just as with crop farming, dairies have used technology and industrialized farming methodologies to make more with less: to increase efficiency and output, maximize profits and production.

But the result of these changes has not been prosperity; it's been crisis. In the last couple of decades, even though Idaho dairymen have doubled their production, they are making 38 percent less than they were in 1980, adjusted for inflation, while dealing with rising costs for labor, fuel, fertilizer, and chemicals.[25] Dairies worry about the same issues of consolidation, monopolization, overproduction, and rising costs that their crop-farming peers are struggling with. And none of this takes into account the ecological toll this massive milk production has had on nearby rivers, groundwater, and reservoirs due to the combined runoff caused by feedlots' nitrogen, phosphorus, and antibiotic-heavy manure and by fertilizers used in fields.[26]

I first talked to Lucy about her dairy in 2015. But as milk prices plummeted and dairies across the United States went under, her enthusiasm for the work waned—not because she didn't love the dairy, but because she knew she and Joe couldn't keep up. They were struggling with low prices, the stress of their work, and the difficulty of finding good workers. The cows take no days off, and so farmhands have to be present every day to care for them. Workers must feed the cows and give them fresh, clean water (some farmers rotate their cows on fresh pasture, whereas others—Lucy and Joe included—supply their cattle with grain, corn silage, and hay feed). They must clean the feeding, staying, and milking areas of the dairy on a daily basis, replacing soiled bedding so that the cows do not develop mastitis or other illnesses. Milking equipment has to be kept clean so that the milk is hygienic. The cows have to be up-to-date on vaccinations as well as deworming and delousing programs. And dairy cows generally need to be milked twice a day (once every twelve hours), seven days a week.

Lucy and Joe have employed undocumented immigrants on their dairy farm in the past. Like many other farmers in Idaho, they've seen the work ethic and reliability of these workers, who often come to work for a season and then travel home with their earnings. These workers, one dairyman told a local Idaho news channel, "are our best employees. They're loyal, they show up for work and they do the job."[27] Rick Naerebout, CEO of the Idaho Dairymen's Association, said in 2020 that he believes about 90 percent of workers in the Idaho dairy industry were born outside the United States.[28]

As the Boise area continues to grow exponentially, some local migrants are leaving agricultural work for construction work, according to several farmers and orchard owners I talked to. Work on a construction site may pay similarly, but the hours are often better, and the jobs are less seasonal than crop and fruit farming.

Many farmers in the United States may struggle with powerlessness in the face of corporate control, but farmworkers are at the bottom of the agricultural food chain and bear the brunt of the system's current injustices. Farms and agribusinesses across the United States have taken advantage of undocumented laborers, paying them unfairly and refusing to offer them benefits, health insurance, overtime, or days off. Field-workers on many large farms are at high risk of injury, heat stress, and pesticide-related illness. As the *Los Angeles Times* reported in 2016, farmworkers are some of "the least politically powerful employees in the nation."[29] The U.S. Department of Labor's National Agricultural Workers Survey found that farmworkers' average annual incomes ranged from

$12,500 to $14,999.[30] Yet, despite unfair pay and instances of maltreatment and poor work conditions, many farmworkers avoid protest or pushback. They fear losing their jobs, their homes, or even being deported.

Lucy and Joe sympathize with the plight of undocumented laborers, because they were once undocumented themselves. After they decided to stay here in the United States, they became legal residents. But they recognize in many of their farmworkers the same determination and hope they had as a young married couple pursuing their dream.

"Lots of people used to come for six months, work hard, save their money, go back home, and support their families," she explains. "But now, it's very rare to find people that are illegal in farming. A lot less are coming."

In addition to decreased numbers, Lucy and Joe found that fewer and fewer laborers—be they natives to this area or migrant workers—are interested in the hours and work required on a dairy. Lucy says they always tried to pay a fair wage and were willing to negotiate with workers. But dairy work involved weekend hours and little vacation time. Neither of those requirements appealed to the folks they needed to hire. A few times, workers simply stopped showing up to work: Lucy and Joe called them to find out they'd acquired a job somewhere else and weren't planning to come back.

There is little prospect of upward mobility for the average farmhand as such—few promises of promotions, retirement, or vacation time the way there might be at a traditional company. For the farmhand who could save up enough funds via work to purchase land, there might be a good deal of interest in getting practical experience on the farm, stewarding the land and caring for animals. Alas, it is likely impossible for the average farmhand today to save up enough to purchase their own farm property—let alone all the equipment, animals, feed, and other supplies necessary to run it. Farm wages are far too low, the cost of land far too high. What Lucy and Joe were able to accomplish more than thirty years ago increasingly feels like an impossibility.

Lucy always had a gift with the cows and loved caring for them. When the Lourencos' first son was born, the dairy's calves began to get sick, and Joe couldn't figure out how to cure them. He hired a nanny so that Lucy could help him in the barn, and she nursed the calves back to health. Many times, a cow began birthing in the middle of the night, prompting Lucy to pull her boots on over her pajamas and head outside. She always kept their bedroom window open a crack, no matter the weather, just so she could keep an ear peeled for any cries of distress.

Instead of aspiring to a home in the suburbs with a two-car garage, a couple of steady nine-to-five jobs, and every weekend off—perhaps a more typical rendition of the American Dream—the Lourencos dreamed of this farm. Their dream required nursing sick cows and birthing calves in the middle of the night, tending crops in the sweltering summer heat, scrimping and saving every penny in order to keep the farm alive. It meant a great deal of sweat and toil, braving the roller coaster of farm ownership in today's economy. It required bravery, agility, and business savvy.

But it's also meant working on land they own, developing a

business they feel pride in, and living in a place where they can watch the sun rise, apricot and lavender, over the distant hills every morning. When I talk to Lucy, I can hear the affection in her voice for this land, this work.

"It's a stressful business, because you never know what tomorrow's going to bring you," she says. "You go two steps forward, one back, and you can make it. I could see Joe with a cane out there someday, still farming. But you do get tired."

⚘

Emmett farmers have grown crops for agribusiness from the very beginning. Many farmers in this area originally began growing alfalfa for local ranchers like Andy Little, who sought more field-grown grasses for their animals in response to the restrictions imposed by the Taylor Grazing Act of 1934. Farmers like Grandpa Dad grew sugar beets for the Utah-Idaho Sugar Company's factory in nearby Nampa. Many farmers in this valley now grow corn for Lansing Trade Group or teff for the Teff Company. Even as their equipment and methodologies have changed, their planting seasons follow similar rhythms.

But there is a deeper disconnect between the farmers and their clientele than there once was. The agribusiness and community supports that once resided in Emmett itself have all but disappeared. Many of the local workers who farmers relied on have gone. Most farmers now have to go farther afield for contracts, equipment repairs, supplies, and labor.

Meanwhile, monopolization in the dairy and seed industries has threatened farmers' ability to make a living. In today's industrialized economy, farmers like the Lourencos and their workers are always at the bottom of the supply chain. When prices plummet, or agribusinesses consolidate, they are hurt the most.

"Small dairy farmers, an aging population, were some of the last U.S. holdouts against the farming industry's pressure to grow or die—but it's unclear how much longer they can last," Phil McCausland wrote in 2018 for *NBC News*.[31] Joe Schroeder, a representative for Farm Aid, said that "the best advice I can give to these folks, dairy farmers, is to sell out as fast as you can."[32]

Despite these difficulties, however, many farmers on the bench are still sticking in place. The Lourencos have always displayed the same self-sufficiency and grit that Grandpa Dad had—the same characteristics that enabled him to farm through the Great Depression and live his entire life on this land. With every seed that sinks into the soil, Tracy Walton also renews his commitment to this land and this vocation, to planting seeds for the sake of the future.

But I still feel troubled. After our tractor ride concludes, I thank Tracy, shake his hand, and drive back down Black Canyon Highway. I see the fields that bear testament to Tracy's hard work and lifetime of dedication, the barn and farmhouse where Lucy and Joe built a new life for themselves. But the more I research what is happening in this and other rural communities, the more it seems that Emmett's future is no longer influenceable by people like Grandpa Dad, who lived here and loved here for decades.

The people who built a healthy place from the neglected, abused soil of a boom-and-bust town will not get a say in what happens to it next. The town's fate is increasingly controlled by distant forces, by cycles of conquest and exodus that erode the empowerment and choice of those who remain.

Chapter Seven

If you drive along the Emmett bench in the fall, you might see a yellow combine working through a field, harvesting teff, corn, or sugar beets. Inside sits Tracy Walton's son: a young redheaded farmer named Terry, along with his wife, Ashley, and their five children. Ashley holds the two youngest children on her lap, while the three oldest boys sit behind Terry with giant grins on their faces. It's crowded but the kids are delighted: they love watching the machine work, love being with their dad in the midst of his busiest season.

Terry and Ashley Walton have done this together at least once a year since they first started farming. When their oldest child was only a few months old, Ashley bundled him up, brought him out to the fields, and sat next to Terry as he worked. Harvesting hours are long: some days, Terry will wake up at three o'clock in the morning, put on his work boots, and not finish working until nine or ten at night. This way, the family can all be together, no matter how busy it gets.

Terry's teff crop is usually ready for harvesting first, near the beginning of September. Although farmers can grow teff for forage, Terry and a lot of other farmers in this valley grow teff for its seeds, which are considered the world's smallest grain (teff has one hundred seeds to a single wheat kernel).[1] In Ethiopia, injera—a crepelike bread with a spongy texture—is made with teff flour and eaten with almost every meal. Idaho native Wayne Carlson introduced the state to teff after he returned home from Ethiopia, where he had been living and working throughout the 1970s. Upon his return, he realized that the Snake River Plain had a markedly similar climate and geology to the East African Rift. He decided to plant teff here and started the Teff Company—a business Terry Walton now works with to market his teff.[2]

White teff is six feet tall, with thick stems and a large head, so farmers allow it to dry while standing and then cut the grain directly with a combine. Brown teff is generally swathed first, dried in the field, and then combined. The combine requires special screens to separate the tiny teff seeds from its stems: per pound, teff contains 1.3 million seeds.[3]

Terry's presence on this bench—down the road from his father and uncle, surrounded by friends and family he's known since birth—is a remarkable anomaly in a nation increasingly devoid of old ties and strong community threads. It is perhaps even more remarkable for Terry's youth: he is one of a handful of farmers on this bench under the age of thirty-five, part of a profession (as well as a town) that is graying each year.[4] Approximately 2 percent of Americans work the land at this point, and of that number, most are in their late fifties, nearing retirement without successors.[5]

As I drive along the Emmett bench, I think about all that's changed since Grandpa Dad's time. The rhythms of the seasons have not changed, nor have the grueling demands of harvesting. But farmers are aging every year, and the agricultural industry increasingly lacks youth and promise. Young people aren't staying in Emmett, especially if it means staying on the farm. Their exodus creates a lonelier, less diverse landscape for those left behind.

Of course, Emmett is far more intimate in its rhythms than many other parts of the country. Emmett is—as local farmer and Idaho state representative Steve Thayn once told me—a "backwater." The fields are too small to use a lot of newfangled equipment, the agricultural operations still far more diverse than many remaining throughout the nation. Irrigation sets limits in this valley: water rights, the work required to tend irrigation systems, and the smaller size of the farmers' fields all have served to slow expansion. The entire valley is hedged in with hills and mountains.

But when I think about the stories I've heard about harvesting on Grandpa Dad's farm, I can see that things have changed pretty drastically.

Like most farmers today, Grandpa Dad cut hay for his livestock at least once per year—proper haymaking enabled him to feed his animals nutrients from the preserved grass throughout the cold winter ahead. After Grandpa Dad cut his hay crop, he would "ted" it (fluff it to allow air and sun to dry the undersurface of the hay) and gather it into "windrows" (long rows of cut hay left to dry in the field). The hay often had its highest concentrations of nutrients earlier in the season, but peak yield happened slightly later in the summer. Weather was also a consideration:

harvesting during hot weather made the hay easier to cure, but rain would ruin the drying process. Cutting hay was therefore a balancing act requiring measured acumen, hard-earned wisdom, and years of experience. Many seasoned farmers knew when hay was ready to be stored by feel alone: the perfect degree of stoutness and ripeness.

Once the hay was dry, farmhands and neighboring farmers used pitchforks to gather the hay and deliver it to the barn. Back then, neighboring farmers all worked together to help harvest each other's crops. They kept books to chronicle the time spent working for and with each other; at the end of the year, if one farmer had worked longer hours for his neighbor than that neighbor had worked for him, he'd get paid 75 cents an hour for his labor, Grandpa Wally told me.

When it was mealtime, Grandma Mom and my great-aunt Helen would call the farmworkers in, welcoming them to sit at a table laden with food. Family and neighbor, kith and kin would sit together, enjoying the fruit of the farm, and then head out to the fields once more.

Harvesting season was larger than the nuclear family in those days because the rhythms and technology of the time required it. Just as barn raisings were once an opportunity to gather an entire community together, to break bonds of isolation and help one's neighbor, so too harvesting was once a communal and associative endeavor. Large harvesting machines have primarily decreased farmers' need for local help in our time. But as conventional farmers' net profits continue to decrease—requiring ever more land in order to make the same (or less) money—the weight of the labor increases, even as its loneliness increases.

I pull up to Grandpa Dad and Grandma Mom's little brick house, surrounded by a square of green lawn. I remember walking through the mudroom with its dirty boots and warm jackets, sitting at the little kitchen table where Grandpa Dad ate his oatmeal every morning. The kitchen appliances were olive green, as was the carpet, and the walls were covered in old family pictures and framed verses and poems. I have not been inside in more than ten years.

When I knock on the door, Terry Walton answers with a baby in his arms. He welcomes me in with a warm smile.

"The house will look really different since you last saw it," he says.

He's right. The front of the house is open and bright, with beige-colored walls and a big wooden beam running down the center of the ceiling. The olive-green carpet is gone, and where my grandmother once hung Scripture verses, the Waltons have hung a large picture of Boise's Mormon temple. But the space is still welcoming and cozy, just as it used to be. Over the piano, Terry has hung old farm implements and nails that he's welded into letters, spelling out THE WALTONS. He tells me they are shaped from some of Grandpa Dad's old farming tools he found in the barn.

Ashley emerges from the hallway and greets me. As the couple sit down across from me, I realize how young they are—they cannot be much older than me, yet they have five kids and are working hundreds of acres of farmland by themselves. That said, although they are young, they are part of a community on this bench that is old-fashioned in its systems, and that has affected their way of life. Ashley still enjoys canning and preserving produce each year, and she quilts by hand the way my great-grandmother did.

Despite the lack of interest many in his generation feel toward farming—especially crop farming—Terry always knew he would become a farmer. His father works the land, as does his Uncle Danny, and his Grandpa Walton was a farmer before them. He savors the long hours outside, the patterns of farm life, the community of farmers on the bench. After high school, he began working seventy-hour weeks at a local welding shop and helping his father on the farm in the summers. He proposed to Ashley, who had grown up in the suburbs of Emmett. (Terry told me he's rescued Ashley from her "urban lifestyle.")

When my Grandpa Dad passed away, Terry and Ashley used their savings and an FSA (Farm Service Agency) loan to buy this farm and farmhouse. Ashley didn't want to farm at first, and so Terry put together a three-year plan to get out. But as she began working the land with him every day, Ashley fell in love with the farm. After that, Terry says, she wouldn't let him quit.

Terry and Ashley grow teff, corn, wheat, hay, sugar beets, and specialty seed crops like radish and clover seed. They have slowly expanded their farm operation over the last several years—both because of the needs of their burgeoning family and because they want their children to have the chance to farm someday, if they want to. Their farm is now double the size it was when they bought it. But they haven't doubled their income—indeed, the past few years they have spent on the farm have been their worst. At the end of 2018, the couple reported that they were living paycheck to paycheck, and Terry was spending seventeen hours on the tractor some days, trying to get everything harvested in time.

"We've been slower to feel the ag downturn because we're diverse, but it's finally coming in," Terry tells me. "This is the worst year I've ever farmed, and I think next year will be worse."

Farming has never been an easy endeavor. Those who work the land have often struggled from season to season, battling drought and pestilence. Commodity farmers have also always dealt with fluctuations in national and international markets, which can quickly turn a season of bounty into one of waste and bankruptcy. This has become especially obvious to Americans over the last few years, as the recent trade war with China led to tariffs on farm products such as soybeans, corn, and dairy. Farmers in this area weren't hit as hard as farmers in the Midwest—folks don't generally grow a lot of soybeans in this valley, and that commodity was most affected by tariffs. Times were still tough, though, and the money the USDA gave to those hard-hit by the trade war didn't seem like nearly enough to struggling farmers.[6]

Despite recent challenges, Terry and Ashley still love their farm, and they love the bench. While farmers are more isolated than they used to be, there are still strands of community here—the ward (the name for a small local church associated with the Church of Jesus Christ of Latter-day Saints) down the road and its social functions bind many of these farming families together, uniting the young with the old, bringing each atomistic farm into fellowship. A few months ago, Terry tells me, when a farmer on the bench was sick, all his neighbors banded together and put up his hay for him, just like they would have in the old days. Farmers work together less than in the past, but their neighborliness has not faded altogether.

I've noticed in conversations and interviews that the bench is, in many ways, its own small network: distinct from the town of Emmett or from other farms below the mesa. Thus, when I ask about young people remaining in Emmett, Terry and Ashley tell me of their peers on the bench. Some have stayed, while some are already gone. Of those who have decided to stay, few have been able to salvage the family farm.

I wonder about Terry and Ashley's children: whether they will they remain on the land, like their forebears, and become full-time farmers. Unless the children of the land receive some promise and hope for the future—unless they know that they can keep the farm afloat and feed their families from it—they will have to leave the farm behind. All the Waltons I have talked to—Tracy, Ashley and Terry, and Tracy's brother Danny—say they will not sell their land to developers, that they will keep farming on this bench as long as they draw breath. But many family names, once full of meaning and history, are already fading into extinction.

"There will never be another Obermeyer farmer on this bench," Terry tells me at one point with a frown. Just as there will never be another Howard here on this land, I think to myself.

✳

July and August are the months during which Idaho's youth proudly don their cowboy boots and parade prized heifers and steers, sheep and goats in front of judges at the livestock arena. Cowboys in training will compete to see who can rope a calf while galloping full-speed, and cowgirls with sequined belts will lead their horses around tight barrel turns. These are also the months when at least some of these youths will say goodbye to beloved pets that are auctioned off for slaughter.

On a few occasions, I sat with my father and listened to the auctioneer at the 4-H and FFA market animal sale, marveling at the speed with which he rattled off names and prices. One year, I watched as a girl—not much older than me—led her steer into the ring with a pink halter. There were tears streaming down her face.

The auctioneer looked at the girl, and said, "All right, folks, this animal means a lot to this girl. Let's give her a good price."

Her sale was one of the best of the night.

The county fair is a time when local youths who are proud countryfolk—who've cared for horses in the cold of winter or gotten up to milk cows at the crack of dawn—get to showcase their burgeoning talents and passions, the fruit of their hard work. It's the season in which we, as a community, applaud their talents and their abilities in this field of animal husbandry and showmanship.

But as an adult, I realized that the county fair and the rodeo are also part of their assimilation into the fabric of local agriculture:

an effort aimed at inculcating the values necessary to farm or ranch once they are older. Even for the most enthusiastic FFA or 4-H members, however, these efforts don't always have their intended impact.

FaithAnn Hynek calls herself an "Emmett original": She has lived in this valley her entire life and spent her growing-up years going to local rodeos and country concerts, hunting with her brothers, and swimming in the Black Canyon Reservoir. Her parents live on five acres of property outside town, "way out in the sticks," where they raised horses and sheep until FaithAnn was in high school. She began participating in 4-H as a kid and would wake at dawn during the Gem County Fair to ride her horse and prepare for showings. She was the 2016 Miss Gem County Outstanding Teen and rode down Emmett's Main Street in a classic automobile during the annual cherry festival.

I met FaithAnn over the phone, after talking to a representative from Emmett's Future Farmers of America program about young people in the valley who were interested in agriculture. FaithAnn was the FFA chapter's secretary at the time, finishing up her senior year of high school. She told me that she has always wanted a career in agriculture—and for a while, she was hoping to own or work on a dairy. But these days, her goal is to work in marketing for the Idaho Cattle Association or for the Professional Bull Riders. For the first couple of years following graduation, FaithAnn attended the College of Southern Idaho, a few hours' drive south in the city of Twin Falls. She then transferred to Utah State University in the fall of 2020, where she is studying agriculture communications and journalism.

When she was finishing high school, FaithAnn told me she was determined to get out of Emmett—and now that she is in college, she doesn't think she will ever move back. When Faith-Ann graduated from Emmett High School, her senior class was filled with folks she has known since preschool, including her best friend, Aubri. The two have been inseparable for the past fifteen years. Even now, as they attend separate colleges, they still try to meet up on the weekends they both visit home.

But there aren't enough jobs in this valley, she told me, and she thinks the education system is rather poor. Besides, in Emmett, "everyone knows everyone's business," she said. "I wanted to get away from the drama." Other places offer her the independence and novelty, romance and success that Emmett lacks.

In high school, a handful of FaithAnn's peers wanted to stay put: perhaps they planned to help out on the family farm or to find a job in town. But most couldn't wait to leave. "They're moving on to bigger and better things," Faith said. "I'm one of those 'I want to get out of here' kids."

FaithAnn and I met for coffee one afternoon during her first Thanksgiving break, at a tiny coffee shop called Banducci's that doubles as a tanning salon. She wore a floral cardigan, and her long, dark hair was immaculately curled. After we ordered our drinks, I asked FaithAnn about her first semester at school. She told me she was loving college. Before she decided on the College of Southern Idaho (CSI), she had planned to attend Oregon State University (OSU)—to get out of rural Idaho and experience something new. But when she visited OSU with her family, she hated it. "Everyone was nice," she remembered, "but I just didn't feel at home. I specifically remember thinking, 'I see no one in cowboy boots.'" Her country roots pulled her back toward her home state, where she ended up enjoying the more rural culture of CSI.

Growing up, most folks I knew remained close to home after high school. And that decision never resulted in any sort of local disapproval that I could see. But as I've gotten older, I've also heard the voices of our larger national culture filtering through, asserting that those who choose to stay in place—or to return to it—do not "have what it takes." And those voices seem to be getting louder as our rural towns get poorer. People who stay are perceived as not smart enough, ambitious enough, or courageous enough to make it in a more urban environment. Their dreams and visions are seen as too small.

Brain drain doesn't just happen as jobs grow scarce, after all. In their book *Hollowing Out the Middle*, Carr and Kefalas note that it is also fueled by "a regional filtering system" that encourages some young people to stay and others to go.[7] Teachers, parents, and neighbors "push and prod the talented kids to succeed," often arguing that these young people will be wasting their potential if they stay in their hometown. In order to do something with their lives, they need to leave home behind. No matter the fulfillment they might feel in remaining closer to home, no matter the health they might build in their small communities over the course of their lifetime, this is how the world sees them. This is, indeed, how many of their teachers and peers see them.

FaithAnn, for her part, once worried that going to a junior college would make her a failure. But her mom, who she describes as her best friend, urged her to reconsider the College of Southern Idaho so that she would be closer to home. CSI was a small and close-knit community, which still offered the separation from Emmett that she craved. There was only one other Emmett student at CSI when she began attending the college: FaithAnn recognized his pickup truck the instant she arrived at school (when you go to a tiny high school in a tiny town, she explained, you know everyone's license plate). The two of them didn't hang out, but FaithAnn told me that if she ever needed to call him and ask for help, she knew he would be there for her. Because that's what Emmett folks do.

Living in a town where everyone knows everybody can result in a suffocating visibility, a sense of always being seen (and judged). But it can also cultivate a demeanor of service and neighborliness that pushes us to help those around us—even those we barely know—because of the ties that bind us together. It is a gift that is easy to overlook until it's gone.

In the mid-1800s, almost 70 percent of the U.S. labor force worked in agriculture.[8] Property ownership carried with it a guarantee of hope for the future, an inheritance that could be passed on to the next generation. Farming always involved commitment, a "sticking," so to speak. But many were willing and eager to make that commitment, and many more immigrants traveled to this country in order to pursue it.

These days, many young people who are in the best position to take on farming—the children and grandchildren of farmers—have little to no interest in agriculture. Perhaps they have grown up observing the long weekends of work, the nighttime vigils, resulting in few vacations and endless stress. But perhaps, too, they—like many of us—don't want to live their whole lives in one place, without any opportunity to move on or move out. Farming, at this point, requires an extremely countercultural commitment to stick. And many people have no desire to make that commitment.

The U.S. Department of Agriculture seems to be realizing—slowly, perhaps—that seeds planted in the twentieth century are bearing dangerous fruit in the twenty-first. As farmers gray and retire, a lack of interested farm heirs, coupled with the cost of land, has prompted many to sell their land to developers rather than pass on the farm to another generation. In response, programs such as the Farming Opportunities Training and Outreach Program are meant to reverse the damage of the past decades.[9] The USDA is trying desperately to woo young people back to the land—and to strengthen the markets that broke down when we began emphasizing international trade to the detriment of local vibrancy. Through FSA programs, a beginning farmer can now borrow $300,000.[10]

But funds offered to young farmers like Terry and Ashley are minuscule compared to those set aside for corporate agriculture's cash subsidies and crop insurance programs. From 1996 to 2016, the top 10 percent of agricultural companies received 77 percent of the Farm Bill's total commodity subsidies.[11] The 2018 bill continued this pattern, proffering enormous subsidies to large corporations rather than prioritizing the needs of smaller farmers.[12]

Many, thus, are hesitant to take on the family farm. Indeed, many are *told* not to—just as they are told to leave rural America behind in order to make something of themselves. There is a cultural prejudice toward farming that often turns the next generation of potential farmers away from the land. Author and farmer Joel Salatin notes in his book *Fields of Farmers* that when he returned to his parents' farm full-time, his friends and mentors "mourned the squandering of brain power." When he told his high school guidance counselor that he wanted to farm someday, "we had to call paramedics to revive her. Not really, but you get the picture. It was not a pretty sight."[13] He believes a cultural condescension toward farming, especially among the nation's intellectual elites, is pushing young people away from the land and its cultivation.

"Farming is seen as what you do if you can't do anything else," he once told me during an interview on his farm in southern Virginia. Even the smart young people who do choose to pursue careers in agriculture are gravitating away from farmwork and toward "ag business"—careers in communications, marketing, or administration—rather than working in fields or barns. This fits with a larger cultural rejection of blue-collar work and manual labor—those sorts of jobs that, in fact, serve as the foundation of our society: maintaining the roads and plumbing, electricity and food items that undergird everyday existence.

But as we confront the perils of climate change, soil depletion, and water contamination, Salatin argues that we "need our best and brightest out there" in the fields, stewarding our land and repairing damage done by past generations. The survival of our food system will require talent and investment: a passion for rural lands as well as for the city, a dream that involves hard labor as well as seasons of rest.

"That so many people think this visceral relationship with life's daily wonders is not attractive or appropriate for technologically advanced sophisticates indicates a profound hubris and lack of understanding," Salatin writes in *Fields of Farmers*. "We are all utterly and completely dependent on soil, honeybees, raindrops, sunlight, fungi, and bacteria. Neither the greatest scientific discovery nor the highest gain on Wall Street compares to the importance of a functioning carbon cycle or dancing earthworms."[14] Farming has not resulted in a "squandering of brain power," in Salatin's opinion—to the contrary, it has stretched farmers' talents and abilities further than many other jobs would have, deepening their knowledge of biology, horticulture, animal husbandry, carpentry, and more.

Just as important, however, Salatin enjoys being a farmer. On his farm, he observes the giddy joy of cows as they move to new green pasture, the relish of chickens feasting on potato bugs from the garden. For Salatin, the work of a farm is a participation in wonder and thus a call to humility and service, to subjugating one's own needs and desires to the needs of the larger world in which we live. It is demanding and difficult, to be sure. But it is also a delight.

Many other farmers I've met have mentioned this same deep joy. Tracy Walton's brother Danny once told me that "watching plants grow, and seeing baby calves—that whole thing is a euphoria for me."

When my dad was in high school, he helped out a lot on the farm, and some of his favorite memories are from those days of hard work. He remembers long days helping put up hay or caring for farm animals. One of his most potent memories is of helping his father and Grandpa Dad "pull a calf" that was birthing backward.

Panting with the effort, all three men stopped to get their breath after managing to get the calf's hips out. But while they paused, while that little calf was still half-born, it began to swish its tail back and forth.

Grandpa Dad laughed, my dad remembers. "Let's finish," he said. "That calf is excited to start its life."

Experiences like this offered my dad a deeper understanding of life, its cost and its worth—and gave a deeper meaning to his own life, as a result. Grandpa Dad's farm was a place he kept returning to, even as he got older, because it was a place in which work and delight, grief and joy, went hand in hand.

"I've helped calves be born into this world," he once told me. "I've nursed sick calves back to health and have dug graves for calves that didn't make it. I'm a better person for my time doing that."

But in the eyes of the world, this work has little value. It's what you do if you can't do anything else. It's a "squandering of brain power," a waste of potential. It's "settling." And no one, in a mobile and modern society, should have to settle. So the children of the land leave it behind, the farmland empties out, and the acres once planted by our forebears go up for sale.

What happens when the children of the land "go far"—when they listen to a culture that tells them they should never stick, never stay in place?

John Lavergne knows. He grew up in the state of Washington, but he has worked as a counselor in the Treasure Valley since 2002—first as a mental health counselor for troubled youth and then with a public school in Nampa for several years. He now works at Emmett High School, and the walls of his office are decorated with graduation pictures and invitations: remembrances of those who "made it."

In his book *Who's Your City?*, Richard Florida classified Americans into three groups: the "mobile," who have the education and means to move to places with greater opportunity; the "stuck," who lack those resources and opportunities; and the "rooted," who "have the resources to move, but prefer to stay where they are."[15]

Florida's categories complement four group classifications Carr and Kefalas defined in their book on brain drain: The "Achievers" and "Seekers" leave home for jobs or education, they wrote, while the "Stayers" are stuck in place with little to no opportunity. The "Returners," like the rooted, choose their hometowns postcollege because they love them.[16]

Like many rural youths, Emmett's high school students could be divided into the kids who stay and the kids who go. But Lavergne said he divides each class of students into thirds: the top third is <u>bright and motivated,</u> like FaithAnn Hynek. Most of these students come from supportive homes and need little motivation or help getting through high school. When they leave for college, they rarely come back. Carr and Kefalas call this group the <u>"Achievers,"</u> comprising the largest source of out-migration in rural communities.

Lavergne's middle third of students often require <u>tutoring and encouragement</u>; many of them will be the first generation in their families to go to college, if they choose to go. Some might express interest in trade school or community college, but many will get a job straight out of high school—here in town or nearby.

The lower third of students is where Lavergne spends most of his time, he told me—and often, he's just focused on helping them finish high school. Many come from troubled homes, where there is substance abuse and poverty. Lavergne often feels he doesn't have enough time to invest in these students and has to refer the neediest to counselors in the community. But since he started working with troubled youths in this area, over fifteen years ago, he's felt a calling to keep reaching out.

"These kids need stable adults in their lives," he told me. "Their home lives are heartbreaking."

Unfortunately, Lavergne is often the exception to the rule among high school counselors. In their research, Carr and Kefalas found that many schools invest all their time and energy into their most talented and promising students, ignoring the needs of the students who are most desperate for investment—the students who are, in fact, most likely to stay put in their communities.[17]

In a phone conversation, Maria Kefalas told me that, over the course of writing *Hollowing Out the Middle*, she realized that "not one high school dropout had left" the community they were researching. Kefalas had studied urban communities in the past and was struck by the parallels she saw between the kids she met who were stuck in dying rural towns and the kids she had previously met in northern Philadelphia. "It was the same disease, just a different variation," she said. "It moved slower and looked bucolic, but the kids who stayed were trapped in this economy. They knew they weren't going to do better than their parents, they knew how the teachers looked at them."

For all these reasons, it's remarkable to consider that, just about a century ago, Grandpa Dad emerged from the difficulties of poverty in this landscape by *not* moving—by staying in one spot for his entire life. But wealth is no longer built through allegiance to a community or a town; it is increasingly achieved in isolation by individuals and grown through rootlessness, not through loyalty. When we lose hope, we move on. When the prospect of future joy and prosperity abandon a place, we abandon it—if we can. That is how a modern, mobile society works. The wealthy and corporate success stories of our world are constantly jetting from coast to coast, country to country, time zone to time zone—and they encourage the rest of us to do the same.

"The new elites . . . are far more cosmopolitan, or at least more restless and migratory, than their predecessors," Christopher Lasch wrote in his book *The Revolt of the Elites and the Betrayal of Democracy*. "Ambitious people understand, then, that a migratory way of life is the price of getting ahead."[18]

But the price of this mobility is paid by those who do not have the money, the opportunity, or the desire to leave: people like the members of this little farm town. Recent census data show that in many nonmetro areas throughout the United States, fewer people are returning home (or moving in) than are leaving, and births are just barely outnumbering deaths.[19] People left behind in aging, emptying rural towns often see few opportunities for their future and lack both social and economic security. People like FaithAnn decide to leave home for good.

Rootedness and perennial belonging often make sense to us on a scientific, ecological level. We know (or are at least realizing) what the soil needs for biological health and flourishing. But there seems to be a widespread belief in our society that these principles do not apply to people: that we are different, that our minds and souls are, in fact, better suited to wandering and restlessness than to faithful belonging, the choice to stick.

Those who stay in place, or are stuck in place, may thus forever fight the assumption that they were not enough, are not enough, to do something "more" with their lives. They will likely confront a version of the American Dream in which success is cosmopolitan and grand, filled with glamour and prestige—not a small or local thing.

When I talk to Terry and Ashley Walton, I wonder what life would have been like for me if I had stayed in Idaho. I wonder if I would have had the maturity to embrace my roots as they have

Success can be a small/local thing

and to try to follow in the footsteps of my forebears. I worry that, instead, I would have been like those high schoolers FaithAnn talks about: the ones who believe "bigger and better things" are always off on the horizon, far away from home.

I remember a quote from Wendell Berry's novel *Nathan Coulter*, in which the protagonist notes that "hills always looked blue when you were far away from them. . . . It made you want to be close to them."[20] But Nathan's uncle Burley tells him that when you get closer, those blue hills look exactly like the hills you've left: "When you looked back your own hills were blue and you wanted to go back again. He said he reckoned a man could wear himself out going back and forth."[21]

I often feel like I don't belong in Idaho or in Virginia: both defined by my roots and remade by my present reality. In her memoir, *Heartland*, Sarah Smarsh says her life "has been a bridge between two places: the working poor and 'higher' economic classes. The city and the country. College-educated coworkers and disenfranchised loved ones. . . . Stretching your arms that far can be painful."[22]

The stretching has, in many ways, been good for me. I can see the ways it has deepened and complicated my vision, given me new understanding, insight, and, hopefully, empathy. But I do feel worn-out, sometimes, going back and forth. Perhaps this is the natural consequence of "going far." Or perhaps life would get easier if I just let go of one side of the bridge: if I stopped going back and forth and chose one place or the other.

Chapter Eight

Emmett has lost more than just youths over time. It has also lost many of its trees: those emblems of longevity and love that helped create a local, connected food system in this little farm town.

Despite this depletion, summer in Emmett still generally begins with the cherry festival. The town's inaugural cherry festival was held in 1928, after a local named Shorty Britton proposed a dance at the end of the cherry season. Interest surged to such a degree, Shorty "got scared" and asked the local American Legion to take over.[1] That first year, the Liberty Theatre and Riverside Hall hosted dances, and the town gave away little baskets of cherries. The festival slowly grew from there until, in 1949, a crowd of twelve thousand flocked to Emmett for the festival's two-mile parade, horse show, live band concert, and dances, "packing the sidewalks from store front to street."[2] As cherry trees sprung up like rubies from the soil, they continued to offer people the hope and expectation they needed to call this land "the Valley of Plenty."

The festival was once flexible in its timing, dependent entirely on the ripeness of the valley's cherries. But nowadays, it is held the second full week of June, regardless of whether cherries are ready to pick. This makes it easier to promote and plan, but (ironically) makes it harder to market the local cherry crop.

If cherries are ready in time for the festival, attendees can flock to the orchards on the east and south slopes of town where gleaming cherries cascade down from tree branches in thick, grapelike clusters. They will sample luscious, mahogany-colored Bing cherries, yellow-and-blush Rainier cherries that are both tart and sweet, the firm Lambert cherries that are perfect for baking, or giant Lapins cherries with their dark-red, firm flesh. Farm stands will offer cherry jams and jellies, juices and purees.

Then locals will set out their lawn chairs along the cherry festival parade route to watch cowboys, carriages, and floats proceed down Main Street. Folks will ride the carousel, visit the quilt show, and participate in the cherry pit-spitting or pie-eating contests. They will go to the Kiwanis pancake breakfast, the car show, the fireman hose competition, and the Jr. Miss Cherry Festival Pageant. And in the evenings, as bands perform in the band shell, everyone will set up picnic blankets and chairs as they feast on hot dogs and funnel cakes.

The Emmett Cherry Festival is an iconic small-town celebration, and one of the last remaining vestiges of its proud past as an orchard town. Its fruit served as a cash crop, or commodity, that local farmers could sell to faraway lands and markets. But it was also a source of local food and feasting: a crop harvested for and within Emmett itself. Thus, the cherry festival reminds Emmett residents of what they have always had in this little river valley: community, belonging, and some of the best fruit around. Perhaps in the future, it will also remind them of what they have lost—of the people, and the fruit, that have disappeared with time.

In 2013, three days of twenty-three-degree temperatures wiped out nearly all the valley's cherry crop and damaged many of its trees, local orchard owners told me. The valley's orchards were already struggling. But after that 2013 freeze, more orchards went under. In 1979, Emmett had 3,500 acres of fruit trees; it now has about 276 acres left.[3] Many wonder whether Emmett's cherry festival will have any cherries left to celebrate in a decade or two.

Emmett, like a lot of rural areas, has struggled to maintain its local food culture. An increasing number of rural areas—even in the nation's "breadbasket," ironically enough—qualify as food deserts because of their limited access to fresh, healthy food sources.[4] According to reporter Corie Brown, the American Heart Association is teaching rural Kansans how to garden because the skill has been lost, the practice abandoned, and health in these rural communities is suffering because of it.[5]

Emmett is better off than most secluded rural towns, in this sense. Most folks here in this valley still have vegetable gardens. Many keep chickens or plant a few fruit trees and berry bushes in their backyards. There's an Albertsons grocery store on Highway 16, and one or two small grocers remain in the area. This is by no means a food desert, and many of the skills associated with growing your own food have been preserved remarkably well.

But outside the annual cherry festival, few folks here have regular, tangible connections to the farmers and the land beyond their own backyards. The Emmett Albertsons carries few (if any) locally produced goods, and the town farmers' market is still fledgling. Most local farmers grow cash crops like sugar beets, field corn, or alfalfa that are impossible to consume locally. Thus, there's a sharp disconnect between the farmers who surround Emmett and those who live within it: a break in a chain that could otherwise connect creators of food with those who consume it.

"Hey everybody, checking in here," Matt Williams says with a smile. "It's kind of an overcast day today, so not superhot, which is good. I'm in the greenhouse, and I'm working on picking some squash for the Ketchum market tomorrow. Our tomato plants are taking over. I did not get them tied up nearly as . . . at all."

Matt is recording an Instagram video, one of several he posts to the Waterwheel Gardens Instagram account every month. Matt points to the watermelon and cantaloupe he has planted along the outside edge of the greenhouse and notes that they're beginning to encroach on the tomatoes. "Sunflowers are basically done, so we're pulling them, and I've got this row of beets that are coming along," he adds. "So we're going to pick some of those today. And then I've got zucchini and cucumbers growing in here, and some more carrots down the way I've still got to pick. And as you can tell, I got behind on the weeds too, but that happens."

Summer on a produce farm is constant work: pruning, weeding, picking, planting, and harvesting an endless cycle of fruit and vegetables. As one crop finishes, another is usually blooming or ripening, allowing the farm to foster a constant cycle of food for its customers (until winter approaches, at least). The Williams family packs their truck with crates full of the farm's bounty in the evenings, piling up boxes full of heirloom tomatoes, peaches, and green beans, and then transports their produce to farmers' markets as far away as the town of Ketchum, which lies in the mountains north of Emmett.

Matt uses Instagram and Facebook to connect the Waterwheel Gardens' clientele back to the land and its produce—giving them tours of the farm's orchard and greenhouse, berry patches and lettuce rows. He shows his viewers what is growing, the work left to be done, the damage done by wind, insect, or animal, and the cycles of growth and fruition that they are anticipating. Matt demonstrates how to thin plums on the tree to get rid of frost damage and encourage fruit growth, and he talks about plant varieties like Prime-Ark blackberries, which ripen early but can produce all the way into October or November. In many ways, his Instagram videos break down the last barrier between the farm's clientele and their food: connecting them to Emmett and its bounty, no matter how far away they might live.

Kurtis Williams, Matt's father, wanted to fix the broken link between growers and consumers of food—if not in Emmett specifically, then throughout this area of the Snake River Plain. The Williams family moved to Emmett from San Luis Obispo, California, in 1994. Kurtis and Roxine were homeschooling their seven children, and Kurtis was working as a woodworker in order to pay the bills. But his first love was growing things: he had received a degree in ornamental horticulture at Cal Poly and helped start a co-op and farmers' market in San Luis Obispo. Kurtis's passion for gardening and local food never faded. Not long after the family moved to Emmett, his green thumb turned into a larger dream: to help feed this valley.

He saw an opportunity to feed Boise's more urban population and to serve some of the region's mountainous resort towns, many of which are just a two- to three-hour drive away. The Williamses' plot of land was not large, but, if well-tended, he believed it could produce a bounty.

Matt Williams was twelve years old when his family moved to Emmett. During their first years in this valley, he often helped his father on woodworking projects and traveled with him to job sites. He has always enjoyed working with his hands, creating something tangible; after graduating from high school, he worked in Boise building cabinets for few years.

But eventually, Matt returned home to Waterwheel Gardens to help his parents on the farm. A few of the Williams children help Kurtis and Matt out on the farm, while others are pursuing other interests—one of Matt's brothers recently opened a gym outside Boise. The youngest child in the Williams family is only twelve, and Matt wonders whether he will love the farm as much as his older siblings. He has grown up on the farm, Matt says, and has never known a different reality. "If all you know is farming," he says, "there's greener grass on the other side of the fence. All you see are the struggles."

But, like his father, Matt loves working in the earth, growing things. Although he knew the farm would be a tough enterprise when he returned to it, he was not afraid of the challenge: he had worked with other small businesses and was well acquainted with both their hardships and their rewards. The vision Kurtis painted—of a valley full of plenty, of a garden that could feed its neighbors—was one Matt wholeheartedly embraced. He describes Waterwheel Gardens as his family's baby, something they have "sold out for."

After emailing Matt and setting up a time to visit Waterwheel Gardens, I drove through the town of Emmett, past new suburban houses and old neglected buildings, on my way to the farm. As the buildings thinned out, I could see the farmhouses and fields that remain this close to town, hugging the curves of the Last Chance Canal. Some cropland still exists between downtown Emmett and the new suburban growth, which is building up around Highway 16, a border of green and gold separating the old Emmett from the new.

Waterwheel Gardens hugs a curve of country road that runs along the sagebrush-covered slopes east of town. The Williamses recently bought some orchard land along these slopes and are planting more trees alongside the old. They've also recently added a greenhouse to their farm, in hopes that they can extend their growing season. Unlike many other farmers I've talked to in this valley, the Williamses' farm is thriving in this soil.

I park and walk over to a little shed next to the family's white farmhouse. Garden plots spread out all around, covering nearly every square foot of open ground on the west side of the house. At a quick glance, I see thick grapevines, fruit trees and berry bushes, squash and pumpkins, and a large bed of brightly colored flowers extending out in front of me.

Matt Williams walks over, smiles, and shakes my hand. As we walk through the rows of plants, Matt talks to me about their operation and his goals for the future of this farm. The Williamses "grow a little of a lot of things," he says, producing a variety they can sell in Boise, Meridian, and Ketchum (home of the Sun Valley ski resort). While they are not organic certified, their farming practices are primarily natural and organic: the Williamses plant specific cover crops for the nutrients and protection they bring to the soil, and they rotate their crops in order to build up soil health, suppress weeds, manage soil erosion, and control diseases and pests. Additionally, they graze chickens throughout their orchards to control pests and provide natural fertilizer, and produce and use their own compost.

In composting, a farmer feeds the land via its own materials. Rather than bringing in nutrients from elsewhere, composting allows the fruit of the earth to then become the soil that helps feed it. The farmer will mix together green and brown plant matter—such as fruit and vegetable scraps, grass clippings, newspaper, wood chips, or dry leaves—along with manure from chickens, rabbits, or horses, if it's readily available. They then provide the mixture with a sunny, moist space in which to decompose. Turning compost regularly will help it quickly break down, as oxygen and heat both aid in the decomposition process, while some farmers and gardeners prefer a slow-composting method, in which they continuously pile on materials for months to a year, allowing the ingredients to slowly decay. With time, microorganisms and beneficial life-forms like earthworms will break down the compost, and the nutrient-rich mixture that results can be spread on crops or garden plots. Compost boosts the activity of microbes in the earth, stabilizes soil pH, improves soil structure, increases the ground's water-holding capacity, and helps reduce erosion.[6] The system is one that symbiotically allows plant, animal, earth, and microbe to all work together to foster health and sustainability in place.

Everything about Waterwheel Gardens is antithetical to the large, specialized monocropping model that has become common throughout the United States. Many of its systems are ancient, derived from indigenous practices cultivated in countries around the world. But these practices are new, in a sense, to this valley, because rotational grazing, cover cropping, and composting, where they did exist, were primarily abandoned in the last century as farmers were encouraged to make their farms larger and more efficient. The resurgence of such practices, in Emmett and elsewhere, is a sign of a turning tide in the world of agriculture: a renaissance of the laborious, intimate rhythms that defined farming centuries ago.

Waterwheel Gardens has cultivated a strong client base over the past two decades. They sell their produce to several Boise restaurants and to a brewery that makes an ale with their butternut squash. They have a market-based CSA (community-supported agriculture) operation, which allows customers to buy into the farm's harvest at the beginning of each year and then pick up their allotted shares every week at the farmers' markets they frequent. The market provides both accountability and community: it connects consumers with their food in a way grocery stores cannot, showing them the vital role they play in supporting local farms, but it also motivates farmers during difficult seasons because they know that "people are relying on them for what they will eat next week," as Matt explained it in an interview for *Totally Boise* in November 2018. "The feedback that I get at the [farmers' market] has a huge impact in why I do what I do."[7]

The Williamses have considered selling their wares at the Emmett farmers' market in the past, but Matt tells me that they cannot charge or sell enough there to make it worth their while—especially when compared to the customer base they have in Ada County. Boise proffers an eager population of city dwellers, alongside a burgeoning population of chefs and foodies who believe in the importance of buying local. Boise's Capital City Public Market has become their community, a space wherein they feel supported.

It seems that farming communities *should* have a high percentage of people who believe in eating locally produced food. And there are definitely some within these spheres of rural America who have become committed locavores. But as farmers have increasingly focused on producing cash crops like field corn and sugar beets, which are not meant for local consumption, rural food systems have correspondingly come to rely on imported goods over local produce. The values associated with eating local have faded as we've weakened (or, in many instances, destroyed) our local food economies. In addition, as rural communities' jobs and incomes have waned, buying heirloom tomatoes at local farmers' markets has become an extravagant and unnecessary prospect to most. It is not that rural folks don't want to support their farming neighbors, but that supporting them can come with a price tag that many will not—or cannot—pay.

Between 2008 and 2012, Idaho's participation in the USDA's Supplemental Nutrition Assistance Program (SNAP) doubled.[8] Eight percent of the state population was enrolled in SNAP in 2019, and almost 74 percent of SNAP participants were in families with children.[9] In Gem County specifically, 13.9 percent of residents—and 18.1 percent of children—are food insecure, according to Feeding America.[10] The national average in 2018 was 11.1 percent for adults and 13.9 for households with children, according to the USDA.[11] And while some farmers' markets around the United States have applied for SNAP authorization, which allows enrolled families to use electronic benefits transfer cards (formerly, food stamps) at the market, there is still a significant price barrier between low-income populations and the foods grown nearest them.

Buying local is often more expensive than buying grocery store produce for a variety of reasons. Because of economies of scale, large growers in places like California can spread their expenses over more acres, which means their operating costs are lower overall. States with a longer growing season like California and Florida are often able to produce double what the rest of the country can, thus saturating the market and keeping their prices low. Prices can also fluctuate depending on individual farmers, their expenses, their help (or lack of it), and where they live in the United States.[12]

But it is also important to note that we've subsidized food in a way that makes local produce expensive. Here in the United States, we heavily subsidize meat, poultry, sweets, fats, and oils—while few (if any) subsidy dollars go to local, small-scale farm producers. Thus, while the price of the former food items has fallen in recent years, the price of fresh local produce has gone up.[13] Because of this, keeping a local farm alive often takes a great deal of work, agility, and entrepreneurship. Matt, his father, siblings, and two farmhands often put in twelve- to sixteen-hour days during the farm's peak growing season. They travel long hours to farmers' markets across the valley and over the mountains. They have to foster relationships with local customers and restaurants, working on sales and customer service as well as on agricultural and managerial work. They host farm-to-table dinners every year and have put together a commercial kitchen where they produce value-added farm products such as jams, dried fruits, canned goods, and other items they can sell year-round when their normal growing season is over.

On top of all this, they are constantly building their social media presence, posting videos and pictures to Facebook and Instagram showing their greenhouse progress and work on the farm. But the work is a joy for those who have embraced it, who delight in watching green tendrils of life spring out of the earth every spring and in reaping the fruit of their labor through the warm summer months.

"Farming is something you gotta love," Matt tells me—and he does love it. Waterwheel Gardens has absorbed Matt's schedule and talents, his weekends and evenings. The farm is still not where he wants it to be, where he hopes it will be in the years ahead. But he has a long-term vision for this place: alongside his father, Matt hopes to build a farm with a future, cultivating a place in this valley where the roots go down deep.

I wish the Williams family did not have to carry the fruit of that vision up over Freezeout Hill every week—commuting with the commuters, carrying their dreams and hopes to other places. Because I know this community once had its own food economy, long ago.

Back when mom-and-pop stores were all over Emmett, Grandpa Dad saw local grocer Willard Slabaugh walk out of his little store with a Bible under his arm, headed for the nearby Baptist church. He went home and told Grandma Mom that, no matter how much Willard's groceries cost, they would buy only from him going forward. To Grandpa Dad, some things mattered more than the price tag—and supporting his neighbor and Christian brother was one of those things. The couple grew and produced most of what they ate, but he also often encouraged Grandma Mom not to budget the groceries they did purchase in town. "We work hard, so we deserve to eat well," he'd say.

Grandpa Dad's approach to food is rather uncommon these days. At this point in our history, Americans spend less of their income on food than people in any other country in the world, and food in America is cheaper than almost anywhere else in the world.[14] But there are larger costs to our cheap food: widespread obesity, soil depletion, water pollution, animal maltreatment, the unfair wages afforded to farmworkers, disappearing incomes of farmers, chemical runoff, and more. Our cheap food is not cheap, and eventually we will have to pay our bill.

Over the past several years, as awareness of these hidden costs has grown, interest in farmers' markets and direct-to-consumer food sales has grown considerably. The USDA Economic Research Service found that the number of farms selling directly to consumers (via markets, roadside stands, U-pick operations, on-farm stores, or other means) increased 24 percent between 2002 and 2012.[15] In 2015, more than 167,000 farms sold $8.7 billion in food products directly to consumers, according to the USDA's National Farmers Market Directory.[16]

That may not seem like much, especially when one considers the trillions of dollars Americans spend at grocery stores every year. But all those dollars flowed straight into farmers' pockets instead of through multiple intermediaries. Farmers earned 37 cents of every dollar the American consumer spent on food in the 1980s—but today, farmers are making less than 15 cents of every food dollar.[17] Squeezed on both the input and the output side of what they grow, many dairies and farms are struggling to make ends meet and sell their goods. In this environment, the direct-to-consumer model—small though it may still be—could offer farmers greater opportunity for survival.

Many folks say that local food is not enough: not enough to sustain our economy, not enough to feed the world. They might be right. But there are also organizations—such as La Via Campesina, the National Sustainable Agriculture Coalition, and GRAIN, to name a few—that argue that Western agribusiness's desire to "feed the world" has served to undercut the vibrancy and health of indigenous and peasant farmers in their own communities. We have tried to pick winners and losers in the battle for agricultural survival, not just in the United States but throughout the world as well, without any thought to the tradition and self-sufficiency that we might undermine.[18]

Matt Williams will be the first to tell you that you can't eat locally year-round in Idaho, or in most places throughout the United States, for that matter. It is a privilege to live at a time when we can buy mangoes and avocados during cold gray winters, or enjoy wines from France and cheeses from Spain when we visit local restaurants. The goal for most within the farmers' market movement is not to feed local inhabitants entirely on locally produced goods for 365 days a year but, rather, to encourage citizens' relationship with the farmers in their region during the growing seasons that do exist. Often, this can extend to a better understanding of native soil and plants, and even a growing passion for our communities and their needs.

As we have broken down the chain that connects people to the food on their plates, we have desensitized them to the way in which it is produced. Most consumers no longer know (nor care) whether the farms that produce their food are *healthy*: whether the people, animals, plants, soil, or communities that make up our agricultural base are thriving or not. We care about cheapness to the detriment of wholeness.

But the broken chain has also divorced farmers from the inputs that might help them make wise business decisions—not only for themselves, but for their land, their animals, and their community. Farmers like the Williamses are held accountable to a customer base that might visit their farm at any time—as well as to neighbors who live in close proximity to their operation.

Local food production fosters a diversity of supports and limits, and carves a complexity into the systems of production, that many farms presently lack.

It is ironic, perhaps, that this diversity and complexity arises from locality. Many people today see local farming as simplistic, backward, or romantic. But it is specialization that tries to convince us that our world is not complex—that the soil can survive and flourish on a homogenous diet, that animals are happiest when confined in concentrated feeding operations. Locality requires us to deepen our gaze and examine our roots. It requires us to see the complexity of our places and their needs.

Emmett's local food economy was faltering by the end of Grandpa Dad's life, at least in some ways. But the Williamses are planting more fruit trees, sending more roots down into the soil. Thus, it seems that the vision still exists, and the land will not be abandoned just yet.

I walk through an apple orchard on the south slopes of Emmett, along rows of manicured trees covered in yellow fruit. The orchard is immaculately maintained: the grass between the trees is clipped short, and everything is free of weeds and debris. Then there's the view beyond: of the dusty-colored slopes stretching east toward Freezeout Hill, the clumps of neighboring orchards and suburbs, the irrigation ditches stretching toward town.

"Do you generally think of Golden Delicious apples as crispy?" the orchard's owner, Lance Phillips, asks me suddenly.

I shrug. "Not particularly," I say.

Lance quickly picks an apple from a tree and tosses it to me. "Take a bite right now," he says with a grin.

I bite into the apple with a loud crunch. It is perfectly crispy, its sweet and tangy flavor lingering in my mouth with every bite.

An unripe apple is full of starch. Until it starts producing ethylene gas, which kick-starts the ripening process, an unripe apple won't taste good. But after the gas has helped convert all that starch to sugar, the apple has a rich crispiness and flavor. It's perfect. But here's the catch: as soon as a perfectly ripe apple is picked on the tree, it will begin to age and grow mushy. Its shelf life is limited, which can hurt profits and make national or international sales difficult. Because of this, store-bought apples are usually picked just before the fruit has started converting its starch to sugar, and stored in a cold, low-oxygen environment that slows the conversion process. Some sellers will also use SmartFresh, the brand name for synthetic plant-growth regulator 1-methylcyclopropene. SmartFresh binds the apple's ethylene receptors, thus preventing it from receiving the cue that it's time to ripen.[19]

Because of this process, the apples we buy at the store can be up to a year old. Once they're finally in the store and on the shelf, the apples begin their ripening process again. But the process of ripening in the store doesn't mirror ripening in the orchard: the apple doesn't have the same deep flavor, aroma, or nutritional complexity.[20]

As I stand in Lance's orchard, tasting one of the best apples I've ever had, I realize that this apple is the fruit of a long legacy of work and fidelity. The roots of this orchard go down deep, connecting the present to the past. But the fruit in my hand is also a picture of the constant transformation that happens on a farm: the seasons that perpetually move us forward into growth, decay, and new life.

This orchard was once owned by an Emmett native named Robert Benson (known as Bob), who was born near the very spot I now stand on. He grew up here on the south slopes, helping tend the apple, cherry, peach, and pear trees his father and grandfather cultivated. He joined the U.S. Army Air Corps in 1940 but returned to Emmett after World War II ended and bought fifty-three acres of his own, just a few miles northeast of his childhood home. In the 1960s, Bob's prunes were shipped to Chicago, Philadelphia, and New York City. Bob often packed his neighbor's fruit as well as his own, charging half the amount that larger packing sheds charged.

In the 1990s, Bob bought back his granddad Seth's orchard. He built a new house a few yards from the old farmhouse where he was born. He pruned the aged fruit trees his grandfather had planted, the ones his neighbors said would never give him a good crop. And he cultivated and cared for that orchard right up until the day of his death. On the weekend of the town's 2015 cherry festival, Bob fell and broke his hip as he was checking a problem with his irrigation line. He died in the hospital a few days later from aspiration pneumonia at the age of ninety-five.

Bob stuck with his orchard, and he stuck with Emmett, to the very end. He was dearly beloved by his community—considered by some to be the "godfather" of Emmett during his lifetime. He served on the Walter Knox Memorial Hospital Board, alongside

Grandpa Dad, and my great-great-uncle Quentin actually helped deliver his daughter Deb when she was born. The world of the Howards and the Bensons was inextricably intertwined: one of faithful work and love, life both begun and ended in the soil of this little community.

But when Bob died, his children could not take on the whole orchard. So they kept twelve acres of the old property and then put the rest of the orchard up for sale.

Thankfully, that was not the end of Bob's orchard. The trees he planted and cared for were not ripped out. Instead, Lance Phillips came along.

Lance was born in western Oregon, near Philomath, where his father worked for the U.S. Forest Service. His parents loved working the land and turned their quarter acre of backyard into a miniature farm with five hundred rabbits, fifty chickens, ten turkeys, and thousands of gladiolas. Some of Lance's earliest memories are of that hobby farm, and of all the animals and flowers they tended. He was only four years old at the time, but he already had his hands deep in the soil.

When Lance was fourteen years old, the family moved to central Washington, where his father purchased an eighty-acre orchard with apples and pears. He paid Lance to prune the trees in ten feet of snow and twenty-degree weather during the winters. But Lance did it eagerly, because his dad paid him well—he made three dollars a tree, often twelve to twenty dollars a day. In the spring, Lance picked strawberries at twenty dollars a day, working on his hands and knees, and every June he would thin two thousand apple trees by hand.

Lance told me all this without pause or hesitation, quickly rattling off the numbers he knows by heart—sharing the careful inventory he kept, even as a child and teenager, of his work and its produce.

"I hated it," he said suddenly. At first his face was serious, but then he broke into a laugh—because here we were, sitting in a house that Bob Benson built, surrounded by fruit trees of every description, in a county where Lance works as the USDA's executive director. He spends his days helping local farmers in order to pay for his "farming habit," as he put it, and dedicates every spare moment he has to his fruit farm.

But back then, he said, "I did not like trees, or berries, or gladiolas. Dad paid me, and I saved it all. But I hated it."

When Lance graduated from high school and left home for Central Washington University, he hung up his pruners and never expected to return to the orchard. He enjoyed the beer, the social life, the novelty. But when he had to pick a degree, he decided to pursue biology because, he said, "I had done it, lived it." Eventually, Lance turned his biology degree into a horticulture degree—and his decades of work in the soil, growing and tending plants, slowly transformed from a drudgery into a passion.

Lance has farmed alfalfa and run a rotational grazing cattle operation, done custom landscaping jobs and directed a garden food program for his local church. But his first love is fruit farming. So when Bob Benson's son and daughter put this property up for sale, Lance bought it and renamed it Crimson Gem Orchard.

That name now graces the orchard, on a painted sign that depicts the valley's prized cherries. But in clear letters, just below the orchard's name, the sign reads "A Bob Benson Legacy Orchard." Because Lance admires his predecessor and his life of dedication to this place, he wanted Bob's name to remain with the orchard: a reminder of what came before, even as Lance plants new trees and cultivates his own rhythms here in this valley.

During an interview with an orchard owner down the road from Bob's old fruit farm, Lance's name came up. The orchard owner had a few hundred fruit trees adjacent to a new suburban development and, even then, did not think his orchard would last. He had no plans to replace old trees, let alone expand the orchard—yet Lance had just planted two hundred more trees on his property. The orchard owner talked about Lance with a mixture of consternation and awe. How was Lance making it work, he wondered, when all the orchards around him were disappearing?

A couple of days later, I drove to the Phillipses' home—the house Bob built when he bought back his grandfather's land. It was a timber-frame house, with giant windows overlooking the valley, and a cozy porch in the back. Two black dogs ran up to greet me as soon as I arrived. They barked menacingly but gave away their joviality with wagging tails.

Lance came out of the house and greeted me with a grin. He shooed the dogs kindly out of the way and welcomed me into the kitchen, talking fast, his eyes glinting with excitement behind his thin-rimmed glasses. He listed off facts and numbers as quickly as I could absorb them. As he offered me a mug of hot tea, I got my pen out. I could tell I was going to need it.

During Lance's first year doing U-pick with the orchard, four thousand people drove out to Emmett through the spring and summer to pick cherries, peaches, and apples. Moms brought their children, and they filled their buckets with fresh fruit. Burgeoning U-pick operations are one way the agritourism I have long observed in Virginia is finally spilling into this area, helping fruit farmers who are trying to keep their operations afloat.

Lance has started hosting fundraisers for the high school band and sports teams: the high schoolers compete to see who can pick the most fruit, and Lance donates the proceeds from their work to the school. He's also begun hosting an annual cross-racing bike triathlon, which he calls the Crimson Cross, during which local biking clubs come out and compete on a one-mile course through the orchard, raising money for the local food bank. Last year's Crimson Cross brought out two thousand people, Lance said. They bought fresh fruit from the orchard, along with $400 worth of baked goods.

During the fall, Lance sells freshly pressed apple cider at football games and other school events. He also sells value-added products such as cherry and blackberry jam, which he calls Gem Jam. He teaches pruning classes, helping locals learn how to take care of their trees, and educates them on spraying and pest management. He advertises his pruning workshops, U-pick season, and other events on his Facebook page, which he updates with pictures and news items throughout the year. Like his forebears in the Emmett fruit industry, Lance is cultivating a local crop: one that helps to feed and support the people who live in this valley.

Lance's orchard is not organic, but he also doesn't "nuke the orchard" as farmers did during Bob's childhood. The residuals from those chemicals used to last twenty days, Lance said—and they often seeped into the soil, poisoning the earth as well as the air. In contrast, the chemicals Lance uses today are mild, twenty-four-hour residuals, and he uses them with precision and sparsity. Most often, Lance said, organic orchards still spray their trees—they just use a weaker formula that requires more frequent spraying. Lance feels that spraying once, at the perfect time to deter or kill pests, is the preferable option.

As I talked to Lance, I could sense his boundless enthusiasm and energy for this work. Lance is part scientist, part salesman, part activist, part entrepreneur, and part farmer, and he never seems to run out of facts or ideas. He has a vision for this valley that transcends his own fruit operation and encompasses surrounding farms as well.

Growing up in Washington and Oregon, Lance observed the ways co-ops and communities worked together in order to share costs and make a greater profit. He aspires to draw together Emmett's remaining fruit farmers in the same way—to cultivate a local market for their fruit, hire steady laborers, better store and package their product, and share costs and machinery needs. But as of yet, there are no orchard co-ops in this valley, and Lance gets frustrated with the ways in which farmers in this area can be so stubbornly independent and individualistically minded. Gem County farmers don't have the collective energy necessary to help each other get through tough times, he told me. So, instead, most have gotten picked off, one by one.

Lance's background in both horticulture and sales, as well as his childhood in Washington's fruit country, has perhaps given him a unique opportunity to thrive in this valley. Our system has evolved, he says, to require that a farmer become a jack-of-all-trades in order to survive—and Lance is assuredly that. They have to constantly grow their knowledge of the latest technology and science in their sector. They have to educate themselves on government policies and regulations, and learn how best to conserve and steward their land. And sometimes, like Lance, they have to innovate in order to draw employees or sales.

But the demands of farming don't always equate with the paltry profit earned from the land, and Lance readily admitted that he needs his USDA job in order to supplement his income from the orchard. At this point, most of Emmett's commercial orchards are gone. Harold Williams, who owned the oldest family orchard in the valley, died in a farm accident in 2018, and his wife and son have been determining how (and whether) to keep the farm going without him. Another old-orchard owner passed away recently, and two other orchards have been sold to land developers and subdivided.

Yet Lance is determined not to quit. When I asked what he was going to do in response to the closures all around him, he smiled. "I just planted twelve hundred more peach trees. When everybody else rips trees out, I plant more."

Lance and I finish walking through the rows of Golden Delicious apples and hike up the slope to the old canal above the orchard, where irrigation lines provide water to the land below. The dirt road along the canal provides a perfect outlook on the entire valley, showcasing its massive tapestry of trees and cropland, homes and businesses.

Lance stands there, taking it all in, and looking down on Bob's orchard—his orchard. And then he tells me that he wants this place to be his forever home. He wants to work in this orchard, in this community, until his dying day, just like Bob did. He has not just chosen Bob's land, he has chosen his life too.

Most orchards in this valley are hanging on by a thread, waiting for the next generation to take over—or to bulldoze the fruit trees and make room for new development. Fruit farmers' proximity to Freezeout makes them more vulnerable than farmers on the bench to suburbanization, although trickles of development are slowly spreading to the north and west of town as well. Many orchard owners who are struggling, retiring, or just plain tired are choosing to sell their land.

But Lance sees diversity in agriculture—having a variety of agricultural producers raising food for their local communities and for themselves—as a matter of national security, not just as an ecological and cultural issue. We should care about diversity and economic consolidation in our food production, he tells me, because a nation that is not producing its own food is dangerously vulnerable and dependent. Lance cares about local food, and he cares about the impact it has on this community. Like the Williams family, Lance is a transplant to Emmett—but he brings to the town a dedication and loyalty that perpetuate the best virtues of past locals like Bob Benson and Grandpa Dad. In a town where many younger natives are leaving, people like Matt

Williams and Lance Phillips could be the ones to restore and re-plenish a depleted landscape.

Lance is trying to procure FSA support for local farmers, but he's also ruthlessly honest about their chances for survival. Of the farmers on the bench, only three are thirty and under, and he believes "only two stand a chance." He is sad and frustrated about these trends because he sees this valley as the perfect place to farm. "There's nothing we can't grow," he tells me proudly. If there were a market to be had, and a profit to be made, perhaps farms could still flourish here.

Ignorance of the soil and its potential can lead to all sorts of ecological misuse. Some kinds of maltreatment are more benign and easy to ignore: Few Americans will critique thousands of miles of shining green cornfields, which are often beautiful to look at, unless they first educate themselves on the dangers of homogeneity to the soil and its consequences for ecology and local food sovereignty. Similarly, due to our widespread consumerism and obsession with economic growth, few Americans would observe concrete being poured over Emmett soil and feel any sort of loss or sadness.

But Lance Phillips would—as would the Dills, Tracy Walton, Terry and Ashley Walton, and other local farmers I have talked to. When they see the soil being paved over, they know what's being lost. It is important that we do too.

Chapter Nine

᪥

To understand why so much land in Emmett is being paved over, we have to look farther afield—to Boise, which lies thirty miles to its southeast, overshadowed by the rippling peaks of the foothills to its east. The beautiful hills turn copper or sage, mauve or indigo, depending on the season and its shadows. Stegner, in his Pulitzer Prize–winning novel *Angle of Repose*, described this valley as a "jade-gray plain with lilac mountains on every distant horizon." His protagonist, a nineteenth-century pioneer, called it a gift to see this valley "wild and unbroken."[1]

As a girl, I used to spend car rides from Fruitland to Boise watching farmers out in their tractors, and the flat, open land would be covered in green growth. We marked the passing of spring, summer, and fall by the state of their fields: by the height of the corn as it inched toward the sky, the color of its stalks as it aged from emerald to gold.

But in recent years, I've no longer marked the passing of the seasons by fields, but by their absence. Every visit home reveals new growth—but these days, it is the proliferation of steel and concrete that catches my eye. Instead of farms, I see an increasing number of strip malls and pharmacies, coffee shops and restaurants, business complexes and parking lots. This valley has traded in plum trees and alfalfa crops for "fields of asphalt and grass turf monocultures," as reporter and Idaho local Carissa Wolf described it.[2]

The Boise Basin's gold boom sparked Emmett's creation in the nineteenth century. Now, Boise's suburban boom is transforming the little town in my lifetime—and having a similar impact on its roots and local life.

Newcomers from California, Seattle, and Portland are planting stakes in this land, drawn by its cost of living, beautiful scenery, and friendly neighborhoods. Microbreweries and expensive condo complexes have filled downtown Boise, while surrounding farm roads are being repaved to prepare for new suburban communities. The old dairying community of Meridian, just outside Boise, is now a sprawling land of private golf clubs, single-family homes, and burgeoning strip malls. Every year, the growth spreads a little farther outward, taking up more of the countryside—including the Emmett Valley.

Folks who've known and loved this land for decades now tell me jokingly, "I guess our secret is out." For a long time, people seemed to assume that Idaho was an uninteresting, bland place. They didn't know about the mountain lakes and meadows of buttercups, the regal deserts alive with a thousand colors, the river valleys with their quiet farm folk and gentle rhythms. But the Gem State isn't a hidden gem anymore. There's a new boom going on, and it is transforming this valley at a breathtaking pace.

Idaho is one of the fastest-growing states in the nation, right behind Nevada, at 2.1 percent growth in 2018.[3] Some state officials believe it could increase by approximately two hundred thousand residents by 2026.[4] In 2017, *Forbes* reported that the Boise metro area had exceeded expansion projections "by nearly every metric that matters": employment, home prices, wages, and broader economic growth all outpaced the national averages.[5]

In Emmett, acres of trees are regularly ripped out and replaced with housing. Stately new homes with two-door garages and small crops of turf sit awkwardly alongside the sagebrush-lined slopes and cherry orchards, juxtaposed between two disappearing worlds. These new suburban developments spring up along the outskirts of town for the convenience of commuters who drive out of Emmett every day. They ascend Freezeout Hill with the same hope and determination of the sojourners who once descended into this valley: seeking a livelihood, a security, that they cannot find on their own patch of earth.

Rent prices have risen in Emmett to such an extent that lower-income individuals in the community are struggling to remain in their own town. A local representative from WICAP (Western Idaho Community Action Program) told the *Emmett Messenger-Index*, "The RV parks are full, people living in camping trailers in the yards of family or friends, there are several living in their cars."[6]

The average renter wage in Gem County is only 51.9 percent of the two-bedroom housing wage. Emmett workers would basically need 1.9 full-time jobs at the median renter wage to afford a two-bedroom rental in town at present.[7]

"Garages and sheds are not allowed to be lived in," Emmett city building and zoning administrator Brian Sullivan told the local newspaper in 2019. "Though I am sure people are doing this."[8]

Low-income renters aren't the only ones adversely affected by the valley's home market and growing sprawl. The development pattern is pushing farmers off the land as well. On a recent trip to visit my Grandpa Wally at his new home in Meridian, I saw an intersection that had been built as a four-way stop, even though the fourth side of the intersection led straight into an open farm field. It was as if the builders were ready and eager for the farm's demise. Perhaps the land was already sold or in the process of being sold. But as I looked out on the green field beyond, that imminent sense of loss filled me with sorrow—for the legacy disappearing from the land, the roots being pulled out of the soil. One report warns that by the year 2100, Idaho's Treasure Valley "could be completely unrecognizable to the people who live there today."[9]

Trappers and miners brought change to this valley in the nineteenth century, and we've seen plenty of booms and busts since then. But suburban growth and its resultant population of commuters seem certain to transform Idaho's rhythms in coming decades. They are making indelible marks on the landscape, quickly pushing out the harvesters.

I know growth is good: it's coveted by many rural communities and small cities in this time of winner-take-all cities and urban consolidation. But in the process of growth, we could lose our more diverse native landscape to suburban sprawl (a landscape that's already been sorely threatened by agricultural homogenization over the past several decades). We could lose our embedded, multigenerational farm community, with its ties to the land and to place. And we could lose our sense of local, historical memory: a communal memory that ties us to the past, with all its lessons and brokenness, and offers us guidance for the future. When everything is shiny and new, it is easy to forget everything that came before.

After Andy Little—the Sheep King of Emmett—passed away in 1941, his empire shrunk and changed. His son David sold the sheep operation in 1962, choosing to focus on cattle ranching instead. Three generations later, however, the Littles are still the largest property owners in Gem County—and one of the largest property owners in the state. Their land stretches from the dry foothills south of Emmett to the mountainous pastureland outside Cascade. They rent out a great deal of that farmland in addition to running their current ranching operation, the Little Cattle Company.

Moreover, Andy Little's grandson Brad is now the governor of Idaho. Brad Little has worked in Idaho state politics for many years now: he was a state senator for eight years before serving as lieutenant governor from 2009 to 2019. His father, David, was a state senator before him and a member of Idaho's Republican National Committee.

Ironically, Brad Little's slogan when he ran for governor was

"Bold New Leadership for Idaho"—an attempt, some surmised, to distance himself from the long legacy and leadership of former governor Butch Otter, who held the office from 2007 to 2019.[10] Establishment Republican leadership has been an entrenched norm in Idaho for many decades; little seems to change quickly or drastically, even as the state's Tea Party conservatives often grumble about their own mini "swamp" of entrenched bureaucrats in Boise.

But considering the Littles' long legacy of wealth, landownership, and political involvement in this state, there was little "new" or "bold" about Brad Little's campaign for governor. He is a member of the state's agricultural royalty. His wife, Teresa Soulen Little, is the daughter of another wealthy, property-rich ranching family from Weiser, Idaho. When he first began campaigning for governor in 2017, Brad voluntarily released details on his financial assets, which were valued at between $12 million and $24 million the prior year.[11] The family business, Little Enterprises LLLP, is worth as much as $10 million.[12]

I met with Brad Little while he was still lieutenant governor, in the process of starting his gubernatorial campaign. As we sat in Idaho's capitol building in Boise, in a boardroom filled with windows that looked out on downtown Boise's tree-lined avenues and busy sidewalks, he told me stories of the family ranch— of a time when the family still employed five hundred ranch hands, when the cycles of herding and shearing, hay gathering and planting were constant. Brad grew up working with the cattle and sheep and attended Emmett High School. He loved the land and the community, so he chose to return to the family ranch after graduating from the University of Idaho with a degree in agribusiness.

"My dad didn't pressure me," Brad said, "but he fostered my interest in ownership." David Little taught each of his children the value of hard work and encouraged them all to help out on the ranch. When he died, Brad and his siblings split the ranch three ways.

But Brad also recognizes that most agricultural jobs and infrastructure in Emmett are on the decline, and that this decline has caused a crisis in his hometown. As Emmett's community continues to gray, Brad has also noticed a reduction in communal energy and activism. The community's older members do not have the same interest in passing school bonds or improving public works. Brad recognizes the brain drain that has proliferated throughout rural America: his website calls it one of Idaho's "most persistent problems." He worries about the loss of talent and youth to places that can offer better jobs and larger paychecks. After all, his own sons—Adam and David—left Idaho for Seattle, to work as auditors for one of the nation's largest accounting firms.

Eventually, both sons moved back home. Adam began working for a law firm in Boise, while David took over the family business. "But a lot of people don't have those opportunities," Brad told me. He has observed the postindustrial collapse, the mechanization and industrialization that have made job possibilities dwindle across rural areas of this state. He wants to convince Idaho's youths to stay, or to move home if they have left. But he knows they need a reason to stick.

For his part, Brad has embraced many of the habits and ideals of his father and grandfather. But as I talked to him, I realized that just as U.S. agriculture has changed, this farming family has changed too. Their role in this landscape has shifted, from the deep local involvement of Andy Little to the state governorship of his grandson. Some of the past century's changes are positive: Brad and his children have opened a good portion of their land for cyclists and hikers to enjoy and have advocated for public land and wildlife conservation. But in many ways, the governor has left Emmett behind as well—he has traded in its quiet rural rhythms for the Idaho State Capitol's bustle and prestige. His success story does not involve staying on the ranch or in Emmett's quiet valley: it has also required an exodus. The family no longer employs hundreds of Emmett workers; the sheepherders and shearers, harvesters and cooks are all gone. Their ownership of the ranch is largely an absentee ownership as Brad has turned toward politics and his son David has focused on the real estate and leasing side of the family business. I wonder, again, whether the rich local culture of Emmett's past has any chance in Idaho's evolving future—or whether this little town will continue to lose farms, their history, and their culture.

This valley was the perfect place for folks like Grandpa Dad and Andy Little: visionaries with a few dollars in their pockets and a love for the land. But in our era, entrepreneurs seldom flock to villages or rural spaces, especially to those in need of renovation or care. We move to places that will offer us something: to places that fit the consumptive cadences of our time, not to places that might ask something of us. And while Emmett does offer

I moved to a place that asked something of myself

many goods to its present and future inhabitants, it also needs investment and love—a new generation of stickers who are willing to make this valley their forever home.

Brad's father was the last relative to own the family mansion, the "Forever House" constructed by Andy Little. The Littles don't know who owns the house these days. But it still stands east of downtown Emmett. The last time I saw it, the property looked a bit bedraggled, but there was still something striking about the old house. It has a stateliness that makes you curious, admiring. Every time I drive past it, I unintentionally slow down. I think that house will outlast all of us.

I drive back to Emmett's Main Street and park next to the He-Brews coffee shop. It features inspirational quotes and Bible verses on all its walls, a chess board and books, and a pair of deer antlers above the counter. I walk a block west to the Little Cattle Company building and open its door. After a receptionist greets me, I meet Brad's son David and shake his hand.

David is over six feet tall, with a wide grin and quiet but congenial demeanor. He has a poster of Ronald Reagan on the wall above his desk. As we talk, I find out that he went to high school with Matt Williams, and the two are still friends. They often swap notes and discuss their farming operations. There could be no greater difference between the two farms, of course: one spans the Boise foothills, the bench, and the mountains north of Emmett, while the other consists of twenty-five dense acres of fruit and vegetables. But there are interesting similarities between the two young men: both David and Matt chose to return home, to embrace the family business, and to help carry on a legacy they cared about. For David, the legacy is an old and large one, with roots in this community that go back several generations. For Matt, the legacy is his father's, transplanted from California to Emmett, and its methodologies and style are still rather unique in this valley. But both involve a choosing and returning, a decision to invest in this community and to walk in the footsteps of their forebears.

David Little grew up on the family ranch, fixing fences and helping move cattle. Like his dad, he attended Emmett High School and went to the University of Idaho. Unlike his dad, however, David initially left the family business and moved to Seattle after college, where he worked as an accountant. But it took only a few years for him to move back. He missed Emmett: the space and the small-town rhythms, the friendly atmosphere and proximity to family.

"My wife and I wanted to move back and start a family, and have a little more space," he said. After his dad began devoting his time and interest to politics, David took over the family business. These days, the Littles employ a cattle foreman and seven full-time employees who do most of the day-to-day work on the ranch, along with some seasonal or part-time employees. David says he still likes to help with branding and moving cattle, although he mainly works from his office. His sons are still quite young, but they love spending time on the ranch, and he hopes they'll also be interested in the family business someday.

The Littles have inherited a wealth of land and social capital in this area, which means their ranch is far more secure than most other livestock operations in this valley. But when I talk to

David, I hear of challenges that I have also discussed with other farmers in Emmett: It's expensive to work in agriculture these days, and profits are low. It's very difficult to find willing workers. The state of foreign trade and the Farm Bill can have a sizable impact on local farmers and ranchers. And a growth in competing uses can make it difficult to procure or manage agricultural land.

According to research done by a team of economists in the late 1980s, vegetable production is the only agricultural subsector to benefit from suburbanization, while livestock production is often the most adversely affected.[13] There are a multitude of reasons for this, of course—but a primary one is that a larger, more diverse, and more moneyed population of locals creates a greater demand for locally produced goods. Thus, in years to come, farms like Waterwheel Gardens might have a greater chance of survival than many others in this region.

But the Williams family managed to start their farm before the land boom. What will happen to the people who want to buy even five to ten acres in this valley to start a farm? Suburban sprawl is steadily either destroying farmland or making the land itself impossibly expensive for prospective farmers. As the circle of suburban growth continues to spread outward from Boise, pushing its radius into rural spaces surrounding the city, starting a farm (or keeping one alive) will grow ever more expensive and difficult. Unless the Treasure and Emmett Valleys also determine some means to preserve land for the farmers to protect their legacy in this place, newcomers to this land could eliminate the very "foodscape" their presence demands.

Boise's burgeoning population is a blessing to an area that might otherwise continue to lose jobs and youths. It is an answer to the problem of brain drain in this region of the state, even if it does not necessarily solve the problem elsewhere. Greater diversity, an influx of young workers, and growth in enthusiastic newcomers are all promising trends. Idaho's Hispanic community has increased 23.5 percent since 2010, and this growth has had a tremendous impact on the state's culture and economy.[14] For many small rural towns throughout Idaho, the work and buying power of its Hispanic residents are the only things keeping them alive: Jerome County, a rural community just south of Twin Falls, is 34 percent Hispanic.[15] The folks moving into this state usually have a deep passion for its landscape, its community, and its future. Like Lucy and Joe Lourenco, they see this state as a place in which they can cultivate their own American Dream. They bring with them an energy and enthusiasm for the good of this state.

But as Idahoans have observed this rebirth of their land—with its accompanying influx of people, disappearance of old landmarks, and rising land prices—many of their responses have been negative. A so-called NIMBY (not in my backyard) demeanor is all too common in reaction to neighborhood growth. Idaho is changing so quickly, it seems that responses are often more shocked and vehement than they might be otherwise. One *Forbes* commentator who recently moved to Boise noted that it was hard, even for her, to keep up with the changes: "When your commute suddenly doubles in length, the cost of rent soars and your favorite view is suddenly obstructed by another new car wash, it's easy to grumble about the influx of people coming from far and wide."[16]

Visits home are often full of frustrated condemnations of "these Californians" who are so quickly transforming the landscape. Some folks have even called the growth a "Californication" of Idaho.[17] (In reality, only about 26 percent of the state's growth is coming from California; the other 74 percent of newcomers hail from Washington, Utah, Oregon, and Texas.)[18]

Frustration with new growth stems from a variety of underlying fears and worries. Some is likely rooted in xenophobia or racism: Idaho is still over 90 percent white (due, in large part, to the anti-minority policies of the nineteenth and twentieth centuries). In one study, Idaho was rated forty-first nationwide for racial and ethnic diversity.[19] Although both Boise and Twin Falls have housed refugee programs for decades, often providing homes and jobs for refugees from Africa, the Middle East, and Southeast Asia, more recent years have seen a drop in refugee numbers and a rise in anti-immigrant (especially anti-Muslim) rhetoric.[20] Farmers and agribusiness owners (such as Chobani, which runs the world's largest yogurt production facility in Twin Falls) are often advocates for immigrants and refugees. But there was an uptick in anti-immigrant rhetoric throughout certain parts of Idaho following President Donald Trump's election in 2016, as well as a growth in false stories about Idaho's refugee population from outlets like Breitbart and Infowars.[21]

Here, I fear, Idaho could perpetuate the worst legacies of its past: the hatreds and biases that forced many ethnic minorities from the land, that suggested the state should be home only to people of a certain skin color or cultural background. Rather than trying to nurture a diverse local community, Idaho laws and cultural demeanors once determined to create the opposite. Idaho's black and Chinese communities dwindled not because they were boomers but because we refused to allow them to be stickers. And Idaho's culture and health suffered hugely as a result. The legacy of racism that exists in this state, that has kept it from cultivating health and hospitality, must be repudiated and abandoned in our time.

But there are other reasons Idahoans have displayed anti-growth sentiment. Some are warier of the state's growing liberalization, as its population becomes more urban and Democratic. There is a chance that these fears are wholly misguided: reports show that many of the newcomers moving to Boise and the surrounding area are conservative-leaning retirees and young families, folks who will embrace Idaho's Republican leanings rather than push against them.[22] But Idahoans often worry that the influx of more progressive populations from California, Oregon, and Washington will change their laws and policies, and thus their cultural and political landscape. Many credit the state's long legacy of conservatism with helping foster small businesses and start-up opportunities throughout the state, as well as good education prospects and safe neighborhoods—the very things drawing newcomers to the state.

Other Idahoans are frustrated with more simple, tangible transformations: the increase in home and land prices, or the huge increase in traffic throughout the Treasure Valley. There's often a significant degree of economic inequality between Idaho's long-term inhabitants and its newcomers, and that financial disparity can breed frustration or even bitterness.[23] I've talked to folks who have lived here their entire lives yet can no longer afford to buy a home in their own neighborhoods—people like Emmett's low-income population, who feel displaced and outpriced by newcomers who buy new homes with cash, and have money to spare. ~ richmond va churchhill

But there are still others who are not so much worried about growth as they are about the *way* in which growth is happening. The transformation of Idaho's land—from creative to consumptive, green to gray, rural to suburban—is causing widespread concern among members of Idaho's agricultural and food community, especially around Boise.

"As the rural edges of the Treasure Valley continue to fill in, there's pushback from citizens who feel frustrated, don't feel their voices are being heard and feel powerless against the political and economic structures that dominate the landscape," Dan Meyer wrote for *Edible Idaho* during the summer of 2018. "These citizens aren't seeing any significant alternatives to the suburban sprawl of the last half century, and they're thirsty for smarter growth that not only honors our land, history and culture, but also enacts a creative, healthy vision for communities of the future."[24]

At this point, the state's growth is almost entirely low-density suburban sprawl: a type of development that chokes farmers from the landscape and creates an especially consumptive and expensive housing pattern for municipalities. According to researchers from organizations like Strong Towns, Urban3, and the New Urbanism, suburban sprawl has social, economic, and environmental costs that we often do not take into account.[25] Even while the car-centric style of sprawl affects our ecology, communities, and health, the revenue collected via suburban growth does not cover the costs required to maintain it. New growth often creates a temporary illusion of prosperity, but Strong Towns president Chuck Marohn has noted that "corresponding maintenance obligations—which are not counted on the public balance sheet—are a generation away."[26]

The wide, unadulterated embrace of suburbia across the Treasure and Emmett Valleys has consequences that are difficult to see now, when everything is shiny and new. But if the state does not consider wiser growth patterns, many fear that this landscape will feel the impact in future decades. Because rather than experience the financial surplus of a growth in people, jobs, and infrastructure, city planners will have promulgated a development pattern that has, in fact, "buried [them] in financial liabilities"— even as it destroys the agrarian landscape that once undergirded and supported local sustainability.[27]

As Carissa Wolf put it, "smart-growth advocates see Idaho's recent growth as a kind of steroid-induced surge that's leaving a scar across the state's rural landscapes and wild places."[28]

After all, what happens if—or when—this boom dies away? The mayor of my little town in northern Virginia likes to remind folks that you can't get the farmland back once it's paved over, at least not easily. If we lose our farms and farmland, we will struggle to get roots back into the soil.

For their part, Strong Towns and the New Urbanism both argue for more dense, incremental, mixed-use neighborhoods of the sort we used to build around the turn of the century and before—buildings and streets like those that line Emmett's historic Main Street and downtown. Mixed-use, walkable neighborhoods produce a much higher tax value per acre and are far more flexible and resilient over time.[29] Incremental growth, meanwhile, enables towns and cities to keep landownership diversified, to enforce good development patterns, and to reduce the risk of bad decisions.[30] This sort of development would include—and hopefully address—the needs of Emmett's low-income population, making sure that housing options are more diverse and affordable than the current set of options. But because it is neither sudden nor detached, it can cultivate a mindfulness of what already exists, and of what ought to be conserved, in a way that does not necessarily sprawl outward with the vehemence and risk of our current growth patterns.

Taking a strategic approach to growth matters because this area of Idaho is going to keep losing agricultural land and farmers. That is inevitable at this point. The question, then, is not whether but *how much* farmland in the Treasure and Emmett Valleys will be lost in coming years. One Boise State University report estimated that the Treasure Valley could lose between 59 percent and 64 percent of its farmland by 2100—anywhere from 190,000 to 220,000 acres.[31] Much in that range depends on the decisions of towns and cities surrounding Boise, and how strategic they are about growth: how they choose to cultivate well-being and sustainability. Low-density suburban sprawl will continue to threaten farmers' livelihoods unless and until the state's leaders consider ways to preserve its history and resources, even as they seek to grow new opportunities and housing options. This sort of stewardship might happen through savvy growth on the part of municipalities; it could happen through land preservation efforts via conservation easements and land trusts that seek to maintain ranch and farmland for agricultural use.[32] Transfer of development rights (TDR) programs could help in both efforts by making it easier to build dense developments, while setting aside farmland via permanent easements so that it is not developed in the future.[33]

Ironically, the suburban boom transforming Boise started on the West Coast and has pushed itself back eastward toward Idaho—much like the gold boom did. Joan Didion writes about the impact suburbanization had on Sacramento's culture in her essay "Notes from a Native Daughter" in the 1960s: "Sacramento is a town which grew up on farming and discovered to its shock that land has more profitable uses. . . . It is a town in which defense industry and its absentee owners are suddenly the most important facts; a town which has never had more people or more money, but has lost its *raison d'être*."[34] Her words remind me of John Ikerd's observation that most farm towns have lost their purpose in our time. Growth is often new and promising. It's important for growing the diversity and health of this area. But if it isn't cultivated in a thoughtful way—in a way that preserves even as it innovates—then all the touchstones that once gave people in this valley their sense of purpose and heritage will be lost.

All this might sound like complaining. So what if Emmett turns into suburbia? It won't be a ghost town. If it is subsumed into Boise's suburban sprawl, then it will survive. But will it still be Emmett? I fear that a place might grow in wealth and people, strip malls and coffee shops, but still lose itself in the process.

The Dills have turned down a bevy of land developers over the years, all of whom offered them a pretty penny in order to turn their farm into suburbia. Saint John's Organic Farm is mere blocks from downtown Emmett and thus one of the few and oft-approached properties in this region of the valley still holding fast in response to all the transformation. It surely must have been tempting at times—as the Dills experienced pushback from neighbors and government officials, as they worked to make the farm profitable and healthy—to think of selling this land for a hefty sum and starting over somewhere else.

But the Dills will never sell this land for money. They're not those sorts of people. I thought, for a long time, that nothing could make them sell—that no matter what, they would keep sending more roots down into the soil, even as everything around them was torn up.

I visited the Dills in the fall of 2019. Several cats and dogs and chickens greeted me as I walked to the back porch and knocked. Susan was making cheese as I arrived. She and Peter put on their shoes and walked outside with me, into the fields surrounding their home. We surveyed the new water line they're putting in for their cattle, and I picked up soft, dark clods of cottage cheese–like earth that had been upturned temporarily in the effort.

We said hello to a herd of steers that sniffed me with wet, black noses and stared at me from underneath their long lashes. They followed us like curious puppies as we walked across the paddock. We talked about the Dills' goals for plant diversity, their ideas for a CSA delivery service.

But then Peter and Susan told me they are struggling to decide whether they should stay on this land. "To move would go against everything we believe," Peter said. But the growth is all around them now. At some point, it could threaten their ability to keep this farm going.

Susan has a relative in Portland who kept farming as suburban growth proliferated around them. For a long time, they made it work: they offered field trips to local schoolchildren, put together a CSA. But now, after all this time, they are selling to land developers. And Susan and Peter wonder, together, as they survey this farm: How long do you wait? How hard do you work to keep on, to stick, when the world seems so determined to push you out? When all the money and power and opinion are against you?

Farms in this quiet valley were once new and green with hope. The soil was good, the water plentiful. The winters were usually mild. From the earth, men and women were determined to build a web of life—a tapestry of field and pasture, coop and garden, house and barn and stable. Julia Freegood, assistant vice president of programs with American Farmland Trust, once called this valley's soil "the crème de la crème of agricultural land."[35] It is rich, diverse, and full of promise. In the past, it cultivated Walter Sisler's apples, Bob Benson's cherries, Grandpa Dad's sweet corn and beef. Each of these farmers, in their turn, cultivated life in this valley: a robust neighborliness, a love of hard work, and a determination to give back. The Dills are part of this heritage, and they have been determined to keep it alive, to be stickers in this land.

Without systemic change, however—without a revaluing of the soil, of all the life that depends on it, of the farmers who cultivate and steward it—I fear that sticking might not even be enough. Too much has changed. Too much has been lost.

Chapter Ten

My family's story—the farm not passed down, lost after its owner's death—is not uncommon in the world of agriculture. Succession planning has always been difficult for family farms, likely even to cause rifts when the subject comes up in conversation. This is probably true of most family-owned business, but the difficulties may be compounded in the realm of agriculture, since the farm is often home as well as business—a place where one's geography, culture, passion, and labor all intersect. In addition, many farmers are like Grandpa Dad: independent mavericks, whose independence allows them to survive but can also be their downfall.

Individualism and the farmer are deeply tied together in the United States, long part of our philosophical and political legacy. Indeed, from our founding, many historic agrarian writers emphasized the farm's independence over its connectedness. As John Opie writes in his book *The Law of the Land*, "Americans made the private family farm into a national icon. It has been long esteemed in the United States as the place where the patriotic frontier and rural virtues of rugged individualism, hardworking industriousness, and personal self-sufficiency were practiced best."[1]

A dangerous tension has always existed between American individualism and the neighborliness required for communal and agricultural flourishing. As professor and sociologist Robert Nisbet warned in his book *Quest for Community*, liberalism's emphasis on the "discrete individual—autonomous, self-sufficing, and stable" fostered an attitude that focused on emancipating man from his communal responsibilities and relationships, in which he "could develop illimitably his inherent potentialities."[2] Some farming communities today feel like this truth unfurled: giant operations farming across vast expanses of land, spanning six thousand, fifteen thousand, even thirty thousand acres. They are illimitable and alone.

But dependability—of people and places and things—has historically served as the bedrock of our little Idaho community. I observed it in day-to-day rhythms: in the soft light of my dad's lamp as he worked till four in the morning amid tax season, or the sound of Grandpa Wally pulling on his boots and heading off to the farm at that same early hour during the harvest.

As well as dependability, generosity was essential to our world: It helped form a community that cared for its members in times of hardship. When babies got sick, kids broke bones, or parents lost jobs, someone was always there to bring a meal, to pray, to offer a helping hand.

The Sislers once opened up their farm to families left bereft by the Great Depression. Grandma Mom organized church functions, visited folks at the local nursing home, volunteered with the hospital auxiliary board, and made cinnamon rolls for families who lost a loved one. Grandpa Dad served on the Church of the Nazarene District Advisory Board, the local Emmett Nazarene Church Board, the Emmett Irrigation Board, the Federal Land Bank Board, and the Walter Knox Memorial Hospital Board. He would often come in dirty from a long workday on the farm and head straight for the shower to clean up so he could attend a local meeting. Life was a given thing: poured out and then offered back in a list of dependencies and debts so long, it could never be settled. It was never meant to be.

Alexis de Tocqueville wrote that free institutions—"little platoons," as English politician and philosopher Edmund Burke called them—could encourage Americans to congregate and serve one another, despite their individualism. This, he suggested, would prevent them from becoming completely atomistic or isolated:

> To win the love and respect of the population that surrounds you, a long succession of little services rendered, obscure good offices—a constant habit of benevolence, and a well-established reputation of disinterestedness—are necessary. Local freedoms, which make many citizens put value on the affection of their neighbors and those close to them, therefore constantly bring men closer to one another, despite the instincts that separate them, and force them to aid each other.[3]

This passage perfectly describes the Grandpa Dad I've come to know, both through my own memories and through the memories of others. It also defines Emmett rather perfectly: as a place full of maverick entrepreneurs, and as a town historically characterized by community, givenness, and mutual support. This farm town held a tension within itself that—so long as it was balanced—gave a lot of support and dynamism to its population. The individualistic tendencies of its people were balanced by their dependability and generosity: their "sticker mentality," one might say.

During and after World War II, prices for land got a lot better, and Grandpa Dad thought about growing his farm in response. But, instead, he ended up getting involved with the GI Bill's Institutional On-Farm Training Program as an "itinerant teacher." The program aimed to help war veterans get started on their own farm, via regular classes on issues like soil fertility, dairy production, and irrigation.

Grandpa Dad could have grown his farm. However, he decided to use his time to give back to the next generation of farmers—to help them get their start on the land, just as he had received help so many years ago. Along with Grandma Mom, he remained a part of the communal chain that bound him to place: made up of the local townspeople he served and worshipped with, the farmers he shared labor and equipment with, and the generations that came before and after him. Grandpa Dad and Grandma Mom were part of a town that supported them, even as they supported it. They were part of a church that served them, as they served it. And they were part of a larger farming community, out there on the bench, that turned strangers into kin. They did not see themselves as cogs in an "infinitely complex economic machine" but, rather, as members of their place: living partici-pants of a reciprocal community.

There is a catch, however.

Grandpa Dad did indeed cultivate a "constant habit of benevo-lence." But Tocqueville also wrote that Americans "are in the habit of always considering themselves in isolation, and they willingly fancy that their whole destiny is in their hands."[4] And I've realized over time that this is a perfect description of Grandpa Dad as well.

Even though he lived a remarkably rooted life, Grandpa Dad was also one of Idaho's original mavericks: the sort of person who helped define the state's extremely independent spirit. He farmed differently than his peers, loved working alone, and re-fused "government handouts" in the form of subsidies. I have always admired his tenacity. He was an extraordinary person: someone in whom hardship, faith, and community built the per-fect foundation for success. But as I have worked on this book, I've come to realize that Grandpa Dad's staunch self-sufficiency prevented him from sharing his farm with the next generation.

Following Grandma Mom's death sometime in the 1980s, Grandpa Dad's brother Quentin (the doctor) called my Grandpa Wally and asked him to return to the farm.

"I think your dad needs you," Quentin said. Without Iva there, he feared Grandpa Dad would grow too lonesome and isolated.

At the time, Grandpa Wally was serving as the president of a local bank. He had worked with my Grandma Elaine in the bank-ing world for thirty-plus years, starting out as a teller and slowly working his way up to the top. But Grandpa Wally also enjoyed working the land, and he was ready for a change. So he left his job at the bank, bought a property next to Grandpa Dad, and began commuting to the Emmett bench every day.

"But if I could go back," Grandpa Wally once told me, "I don't know if I'd do it again."

I had never heard him say that before, and, in the moment, it stunned me. I remembered watching Grandpa Wally walk through the door with mud on his boots and overalls, belting out an old Gospel hymn with a grin on his face—or the times we shucked corn together, and he sat listening to his father's stories. I couldn't picture him apart from this identity as farmer, and as farmer's son.

But Grandpa Wally explained that Grandpa Dad didn't end up wanting his help. The same tenacity and independence that helped Grandpa Dad build a successful farm for so many years—the same grit that got him through the Depression and drove him to build a self-sustaining farm—now led him to assure his son that he could get along on his own.

Grandpa Wally persisted in helping his father anyway, but it often made their relationship as co-farmers—not to mention as father and son—quite difficult.

After talking to other family members and relatives, I came to see that Grandpa Dad's fierce independence was likely part of the reason our family no longer belonged to Emmett, or to the farm. Of course, upward mobility—the slow growth of education and job acclaim from generation to generation—had also influenced this. So, too, did farm policies and transformations, which meant that a farm's income and profit rarely could support multiple generations within a family (these days, few farms can support even one family without some outside income).

But Grandpa Dad wanted to work alone—which means there was no succession plan and no real effort to involve his sons or grandsons in the farming enterprise. The farm was always distinctly *his*: something others helped with but were never integrated into. My father loved helping Grandpa Dad on the farm. I grew up hearing his stories about his efforts working with the calves and harvesting hay, participating in the farm's seasons and work. But Grandpa Dad was stubbornly independent. He did not take advice easily, and he rarely (if ever) consulted his sons on business decisions. He didn't tell them why he irrigated the land the way he did or why he used ditch bank calves. While he was eager to share many of the treasures he had stored up over time— stories, histories, and poems, in particular—the farm always remained something he kept to himself.

When I first began researching U.S. agriculture, I focused on family farming in isolation: the passing on of land from parent to son or daughter, the continuous strand of family that meant the land would not be lost to development or waste. But the more I researched, read, and talked to farmers, the more I realized that the family is just one form of membership, and all forms are deeply integral to human flourishing—including the flourishing of the farm.

The farmer needs neighbors. The farmer needs the church.

The farmer needs associations, societies, and boards. The farmer needs mentors and mentees. When a farm community is working, it is neighborly and multigenerational: made up of farmers who are training the next generation, be they sons and daughters or completely unrelated young people with a thirst for the land. A farming community is a membership that preserves culture in place: remembering the past and carrying it forward into the future. It is a membership in which conservation is linked to innovation, in which we preserve and protect even as we create.

For decades, however, the farm lobby and the USDA have emphasized the picture of the nuclear family, the independent farm owner, and the private nature of farm production—with no mention of the communities that also ought to undergird them. Many of the problems we're seeing in rural America today stem not just from the struggles of individual farmers but from the collapse of the larger ecosystems that once nourished them. Nisbet predicted in *Quest for Community* that when local and associative forms of society are lost, society will become "an aggregate of atoms held rigidly together by the sovereign will of the State alone."[5] And there's not a much better description of today's system of nuclear farm families and their dependence on the federal government for survival. According to crop scientist Dr. Sarah Taber, our American fixation on the family farm ignores the support structures that make diverse, sustainable agriculture work (and hides the brokenness and bigness of our current system). As she wrote in 2019 for *New York* magazine:

Family farming isn't just difficult. It's so brittle that it only makes a viable livelihood for farmers when land is nearly valueless for sheer lack of people. In areas where family farming has persisted . . . it's largely thanks to extensive, modern technocratic government interventions like grants, guaranteed loans, subsidized crop insurance, free training, tax breaks, suppression of farmworker wages, and more. Family farms' dependence on the state is well understood within the industry, but it's heresy to talk about it openly lest taxpayers catch on. I think it's time to open up, because I don't think a practice that needs that much life support can truly be considered "sustainable."[6]

From its very beginning, the American farm has never been reliant on family bonds alone: it has demanded a village. Farmers need more than private free enterprise; they need a collaborative, supportive system that helps with input, infrastructure, and maintenance costs, serves to promote and support diversification, and provides the cultural and communal support farms need on a spiritual, social basis. We see these sorts of collaborative farming groups pop up in response to religious belief systems such as the Hutterites and the Amish. Emmett, meanwhile, was forced to forge some of these tight-knit, collaborative bonds because of the demands of irrigation.

That isn't to say that irrigation in this valley was or is perfect: there's still much work that could be done to make the system more sustainable, both for the farmers and for the wildlife that depend on it. But as an instance of private-public collectivization, as well as communal (rather than atomistic) thinking, it serves as an interesting and important example. Early technologies encouraged communal rhythms, which helped in the creation of farm villages. The cost and risk involved in farming traditionally urged farmers to rely on one another. Industry clusters, such as the agribusinesses that once existed in Emmett, fostered collective work and profit.

To bring back health, therefore, we need systemic change of the sort that will enable us to fight harmful monopolies, strengthen local economic sovereignty, and foster the health of rural communities once more.

Despite all the money that flows to "Big Ag" in the United States, the Farm Belt continues to struggle. In recent years, American farmers have borne slumping prices for corn, wheat, and other commodities caused by a glut of grain worldwide. *The Wall Street Journal* warned in early 2017 that "the next few years could bring the biggest wave of farm closures since the 1980s."[7] In 2019, USDA secretary Sonny Perdue insisted that U.S. agriculture should depend on global trade—even though trade renegotiations with Canada and Mexico, as well as a crippling trade war with China, pushed many farmers to the brink of bankruptcy and even suicide.[8]

As Emmett's communal threads wear away, I fear that only the siren call of individualism (and its resultant isolation) will be left. And that lonely individualism is far more dangerous than you might think. In 2019, the American Farm Bureau Federation reported that 91 percent of farmers and farmworkers were experiencing financial issues that affected their mental health, and 87 percent feared losing their farms.[9] In recent years, farmer suicides and depression have escalated to alarming rates. The consequences of policies that emphasize individualism and isolation are not just visible in economic difficulty. Because the farm transcends economics, and touches on the entirety of one's life—culture, ecology, lifestyle, and health—the downfall of the farm often also has emotional, communal, and even spiritual consequences for its owners. This is a problem that cannot be fixed with money alone: a profitable farm, if it is a lonely endeavor, can still foment anxiety and stress, and isolation.

Perhaps even more than current economic difficulties, these emotional and mental crises reveal the cost of broken farm communities as well as our desperate need for more sustainable forms of agriculture. The federal government continues to emphasize specialization and exponential growth, and the "get big or get out" orthodoxy still reigns supreme. But there is very little resilience or diversity left in many farm communities. Farmers' share of the food dollar keeps trending toward zero. Our government and society have both emphasized profit, the discrete individual, absentee ownership, and placelessness to the detriment of farm communities everywhere.

These policies will continue to hurt farmers nationwide until something changes. Over the past century, they have led us to where we are now: to a nation of aging, isolated, and dwindling farmers; a generation of young people who don't want to farm; and a history of minority farmers either being prevented from farm ownership or being robbed of their land.[10] Agribusiness has monopolized and consolidated power to such a degree that farmer choice and sustainability are increasingly constrained and put under pressure.

When I first started writing about the struggles of family farmers, a fellow conservative journalist asked me warily whether my finished project would advocate for government handouts to small farms.

"No, absolutely not," I assured him. At that point, I was still deeply attached to the lessons I had been taught in college about free-market capitalism and limited government—and blissfully ignorant of the control and influence the federal government and big business already had on these farms.

But now, I believe the dichotomy represented in the journalist's comments—either "hand out" money to these folks or leave their fate to the whims of global trade and big business—is a rather poor illustration of our choices. As a reminder, we already give handouts to farms, but we generally give them to the nation's largest farms.[11] Most folks agree that this is a messed-up system. But they aren't sure how best to change it. Should we just stop giving subsidies to the nation's large farms, and leave it at that? Should we use the funds freed up by that switch to nurture the small and midsize farms we've disincentivized and weakened for generations now?

The problem with pure passivity going forward—removing subsidies and then waiting to see what happens—is that it suggests our rural ecosystems will naturally restore themselves without stewardship or care. And while it might be true that nature would heal much of its own ground if we were to just wait long enough, I wonder whether we have enough time to try that method. Extraction of local resources has left an incredible dearth of health in our own time—and as we are confronting the magnitude of climate change, it seems only wise to assist in the work of building back health and restoring what's broken.

I am not at all opposed to the government using some of the funds traditionally given to the nation's largest farms in order to rectify some of the hollowing out we are seeing in our farm towns. Attempts by the USDA to get a younger, more diverse, and more sustainable population onto the land—especially after more than a century of efforts that were purposefully designed to cultivate the opposite—seems, at the very least, like a more equitable use of public funds.

But it can't stop there—because the problem with the whole idea of "handouts" to individual farm families is that it focuses on propping up a broken system. It emphasizes individual farming families without looking at their larger context and communities. Author and professor Patrick Deneen has suggested that we should instead use public funds and efforts to undergird civil associations: investing not just in individuals, but also in the groups and networks that support them.[12] And I wonder whether that might, in fact, be a way to staunch and heal some of the losses farm towns like Emmett have experienced over the past several decades. Such efforts could involve preserving and protecting farmland via agricultural easements, providing "land links" that help pass land down from one generation of farmers to the next, connecting Future Farmers of America participants with local farmers, helping revitalize downtowns, investing in their farmers' market and CSA programs, and more.

Reform could also happen through efforts aimed at investing capital in stewardship and long-term care, rather than in temporary profit: an effort on the part of the USDA, for instance, to invest the majority of its funds in regenerative programs rather than in cash crop subsidies. Such an effort would make a massive statement about our priorities as a country: whether we want to encourage short-term profit or long-term fidelity and health. It would require people to stay in place and cultivate something for the long haul. It could also turn our gaze again from the focus on profit, which so often creates boomers and destroys roots, to the focus on virtues that increase the health and vitality of our places.

Free-market capitalism and liberalism in the United States often encourage us to put profit and autonomy above all else. But when we turn individualism and profit into virtues, there are consequences. Since our founding, the idea of agricultural autonomy has encouraged a reductive thinking that breaks down the farm's purpose to fit solely profit-focused ends—and has served as a threat to healthy, whole farm communities. America's founding farmers talked about virtue and freedom, all the while allowing slavery to flourish on southern plantations—often on their own land. In our own time, the lack of equitable pay and treatment offered to many farmhands, the unjust treatment of minority farmers, the poor health of our water and soil, and the inhumane handling of farm animals suggest that the same reductive demeanor plagues U.S. agriculture today. Profit and efficiency fail as teleological ends. They do not always—or often—encourage health.

Many libertarians I've debated with in the past do not care if farm consolidation leaves us with ten megafarms in the entire United States, operating with robotics and drones while their owners live in private New York City suites. It would be more efficient, after all, and take out the potential for human error (debatable, in my mind, but this is how the argument generally goes). Many of these folks don't care, either, if we end up importing all our food from other countries, where it's produced more cheaply and efficiently. Once again, they urge: let the free market do its thing.

I think these attitudes often arise from a lack of presence in or knowledge of farm communities—of the vast swaths of countryside that are rural, farm-centric, and filled with people who love their homeland (and want it to thrive again). That is one of the reasons I'm writing this book: to help people in more urban areas see what they've missed, perhaps, when they fly over rural areas and gaze down on an empty patchwork of fields. It's easy to look at that patchwork and not see the life below you. But as this book has hopefully made clear, that world is (or at least *should* be) overflowing with life: soil, seeds, fruit, animals, people, and more. As Wendell Berry writes in *Sex, Economy, Freedom, and Community*, "A healthy community is like an ecosystem, and it includes—or makes itself harmoniously a part of—its local ecosystem. It is also like a household; it is the household of its place, and it includes the households of many families, human and nonhuman." [13]

To cultivate health once more, we must restrengthen that

household and all who live in it. This is not to say that farming's future cannot or should not include new technologies—but that the best technologies will support this household, rather than undermine it. Even if robotics and drones are useful tools for farmers going forward, they neither can nor should replace human presence in the landscape. Ultimately, farming is not done in a factory, a lab, or a brick-and-mortar store. It takes place in the living earth: in a complex, beautiful ecosystem of soil, seed, water, animal, and humanity—of which we are a part. Thus, we must be active, present stewards of the ecosystem we rely on for sustenance, safety, and community. Health is cultivated through presence, connection, and commitment. Unlike profit, health takes into account the well-being of all the human and nonhuman creatures who rely on our food system. The farmer committed to health might have to take a hit one year if it means his farm will be healthier the next—many farmers who are transitioning to organic are well aware of this cost. But in the long term, the soil and all the life-forms that rely upon it will be better for his work. And that is what we want, ultimately. That is the end we should be reaching for.

Many families "solve" the problem of farm succession by skipping a generation. I've talked to several farm families in which land passed from grandparent to grandchild, rather than from parent to child. Terry Walton bought his grandfather's land after he passed away. Peter and Susan Dill inherited her grandparents'

farm. This avoids the inability of most farms to support multiple families. It also solves issues of division over farm methodologies by, in many instances, passing along the land only when a farmer is either dead or retired—no longer involved in its day-to-day workings.

But it does mean that many of the legacies and inheritances of the past, which would tie landowners and their wisdom to current and future generations, are likely to be lost. It's only with a lot of digging and research that I've begun to understand how Grandpa Dad's farm worked, why he did what he did. What I wouldn't give to go back in time and shadow him, asking questions as he went about his daily business. Who knows what other pieces of wisdom and family history could have been uncovered.

Alas, much of that past is now lost. With time, I have begun to let go of the burden of guilt I used to feel over not paying better attention when I was younger, not realizing what a rich legacy I had. This relief has been influenced by Grandpa Wally's words, in large part: by the realization that if I've lost something, it's not necessarily my fault. But it has also stemmed from my growing realization that a healthy farm legacy neither can nor should be limited to the nuclear family. It is a work of the "village"—and thus, the fact that Grandpa Dad's land and home were sold to Terry Walton, his neighbor's son, is a beautiful and a good thing. By that point, Terry was more a member of the Emmett bench than the Howards were. And Terry is doing his utmost to carry on the legacy handed down to him.

The work of passing down a farm, a legacy of rootedness, is a multigenerational effort. It works best when the old are eager and willing to teach the young, and the young are willing to catch and keep their vision. In our family's case, Grandpa Dad passed down countless wonderful lessons regarding community, virtue, faith, and love. He taught my siblings, my cousins, and me about the importance of faithfulness, hard work, and community service. And so even though he never shared the farm with us, I do see the threads of his legacy in our lives. I think each of us has found pieces and parts of the Howard legacy that we're seeking to perpetuate in our lifetimes and to pass down to our children—even if our more literal rootedness and legacy in Emmett is now gone.

My cousin Cortney makes my Grandma Mom's brown bread and embodies the stalwart determination and generosity of my Grandma Elaine. Her older brother Zach is a savvy and talented entrepreneur, like his great-grandfather, grandfather, and father. My cousin Sammee has the sweet spunk and joy of her grandparents and parents, the same heart for children that my grandmother embodied so beautifully. My brothers, like Grandpa Dad and my father, have the minds of engineers and are constantly tinkering and solving problems in their own career fields.

This does not solve the problem of disappearing farm ownership or the lack of multigenerational vibrancy in Emmett and other farm towns. But even if the Howards no longer live in Emmett, all but two live in the Treasure Valley. My sister and her husband live in Wyoming, a few hours from where we grew up, and I'm out on the East Coast. And that is a remarkable legacy—one that is largely owed, I think, to the work and love of my great-grandparents, grandparents, and other extended family.

They have worked hard to build hope and prosperity for their children. And their sticking in this valley is a testament to both past and present love.

I am the only one who really, truly left. And perhaps because of that, I think I am the only one who constantly looks back toward Emmett, toward the generations of family past who built something in its soil. Living in Virginia showed me my roots—and with time, I realized those roots were not just binding me to my parents and grandparents. They tied me even further back, to those days when carriages descended Freezeout Hill in a cloud of dust, and enterprising farmers dug sagebrush out of its soil.

Remembering, the first book I read by Wendell Berry, is about a young man named Andy Catlett. Andy grows up in a loving rural community and leaves it behind for a writing career, much like I did. He eventually returns to his homeland, however, and begins to farm alongside his neighbors. After he loses his right hand in a farm-machine accident, he grapples with an existential crisis and a helplessness that threaten to estrange him from his community. Smarting from the loss of his hand, he travels to San Francisco for an agriculture conference. There, he wanders aimlessly through the city streets and is tempted to envision an alternate version of himself: cosmopolitan, comfortable, living alone in gentility and grandeur—tempted, in other words, to dismember himself from his community and his place.

But in the midst of this temptation, Andy remembers (or re-members) himself: reminding himself that the "flaw" in this empty dream is "the little hell of himself alone."[14] Membership—in marriage, in community, in place—is hard and sometimes painful. It often requires selflessness and a loss of independence. It requires a whole lot of humility. But it is good. And so Andy "thinks of the long dance of men and women behind him, most of whom he never knew, some he knew, two he yet knows, who, choosing one another, chose him."[15] And, in that moment, Andy chooses the ones who chose him. He chooses to go home once more.

Just as Andy remembered his membership, I remember my own: Walter and Leanna Sisler, Robert and Alta Howard, Grandpa Dad and Grandma Mom, Grandpa Wally and Grandma Elaine. I believe my ancestors have called me to live like a perennial: to put as much life and love into the soil as I take from it. They have shown me a pattern of living that is good and hopeful—one that grows promise for the next generation. But is it possible for me to live out their legacy on the other side of the country? Or am I, like Andy Catlett, called to return?

This is a question I am still grappling with. There are no easy answers for any of us who have left our homelands behind.

Chapter Eleven

✿

Nostalgia can make us blind: It can prompt us to view complicated, messy places with a false simplicity or sentimentality. It can convince us to return home to a place that no longer exists—one that perhaps never existed in the first place. Thanks to the farmers and writers who've guided me over the past years, when I visit Idaho I have new eyes with which to see it as it is. I am grateful for this, even when that new vision is more fraught than the old.

When I look at the water of the Snake River, I see the faulty irrigation practices, fertilizer and chemical runoff, manure pollution, and sedimentation that have resulted in its poor health. These issues have, consequently, also led to the death and endangerment of wild Idaho salmon as well as the compromised quality of much of Idaho's drinking water (among other problems).[1] I worry about drought and climate change and the impact they might have on a state that is so often wary of limits and regulations, on a region that often seems to think its water supply is endless.

On one recent visit to southern Idaho, I saw wind blowing clouds of dust off naked Idaho fields. Our car was covered in the fine particles, the earth that had no roots to hold it down. These bare autumn fields are still common practice in the state, left devoid of cover crops or any perennial roots that might help promote soil health. The dust turned the sky brown on the horizon, and I thought about the Dust Bowl we never learned from, the conservation practices we still ignore.

When I count rows of corn these days, I'm noticing the growing homogeneity of Idaho's cropland, the proliferation of water-guzzling monocultures grown for dairy feedlots that further impede the health of this landscape. I'm thinking about our loss of life: the trees torn out, the sagebrush destroyed, the grasses that used to be shoulder-high to a horse.

The Ore-Ida factory in Ontario, Oregon, down the road from my childhood home, is a reminder of the monolithic food processing and manufacturing companies that so often control Idaho's farmers. It reminds me of the undocumented workers making less than minimum wage, of the farmers who work endlessly for less profit than ever before, and of the local markets, agribusinesses, and food suppliers that have died out with time. It reminds me that for all its libertarian claims of freedom and autonomy, Idaho and its resources are often chained to the whims and demands of vast economic interests and powers.

When I talk to younger inhabitants of the state, I notice their disdain or chagrin over the prospect of remaining in place— notice when they equate leaving with success, bravery, and intelligence. I remember my brother telling me, when he was in college, how anxious he was to get out of this region of Idaho and Oregon, a space that so often felt dead and sluggish to him. I can still see what he means when I go home: the struggling strip malls and dead downtowns, the marks of deterioration and loss that often remain even next to shiny new suburban develop- ments. I understand why he's always grappled with staying ver- sus leaving, just as I have.

My vision is complicated. That is what happens when we commit ourselves to long attention in one direction. It is a neces- sary part of growing and deepening our love for our homelands. Anything less would not be love; it would be idolization, a blind- ness that prevents us from truly knowing, serving, or loving our landscapes.

But even alongside the bad, the broken, and the frustrating, I see much to love. Quiet legacies of faithfulness still exist in this community. Generosity, indebtedness, and long lists of small ser- vices: they still characterize this place. So many of the people I grew up with are humble, fierce, and kind. Their staunch indi- vidualism is always tempered by their willingness to bend over backward for someone in need. And the land itself is stunningly beautiful—more so than I ever realized as a child.

There's the valley with its sprawling openness, the cotton- wood trees alongside the river, and the breath of cattle steaming in the morning mist. I love the smell of mint being harvested in late summer, the way its fragrance spreads on the wind. The sight of the orchards, sparse as they are now, still gives me joy. I love the far-off mountains, covered in pines and snow, home to deep mountain lakes and meadows of wildflowers. I even love my homeland's more rugged and deserted parts: the sagebrush-covered hills, wild and quiet, that I so often thought of as ugly when I was younger.

I cannot even begin to name all the good and beautiful things one might see in this land—things that ought to be cele-brated, shared, or preserved. There are virtues and beauties here: characteristics of Idaho's people and places that are worth fight-ing for.

In particular, I believe that Emmett and its farmers have nur-tured goodness in the lives of many over the past 150 years and that this town holds within it the dignity, love, and work of past and present (and hopefully future) community members. In this way, it is like any and every place that has survived through gen-erations of hardship: it has a legacy that is beautiful, albeit marred and troubled in various places.

I am not out to sell Emmett as a perfect place with a flawless past—quite the opposite. But it is worth loving for its own sake. It needs to be loved for its own sake—not for anything it might do for far-flung stretches of the world, but for what it can do for each and every one of its community members. This is the only way we begin to fight off the exploitation and abuse that have so often characterized our rural homelands. It is the only way we can begin to build places that both draw newcomers and keep the children of the land in place. We must remember and prize their vital *local* vocation—a vocation that ought to remain paramount even as these places serve other, more distant populations.

I want this town and its people to have some say in their fate, and in the well-being of their community, once more—to be able to grow job opportunities, cultural continuity, and local food sovereignty in years to come. I want them to keep alive, and perhaps even to grow, both their farm population and its customer base. I want young people to choose to stay in Emmett, and to thrive there. These things are best cultivated, I believe, by Emmett choosing to nurture and grow many of the qualities that made it beloved in the first place: its strong sense of neighborliness, involved churches, strong local and regional businesses, active little newspaper, vibrant downtown—and its connection to the farmers, ranchers, and orchard owners surrounding it. There will be much to reform. But there is also a foundation here that could be fixed and built on for the future. Maybe, just maybe, Emmett could grow its pool of local jobs, financial resources, and social capital. Maybe local farm programs could help aging, retiring farmers find young people eager to keep up their work on the land. Maybe local Future Farmers of America participants will indeed become the future farmers of Emmett.

In writing this book, I have constantly come up against all the things I do not and cannot know about Emmett, because I do not live there. I have sought, to the best of my ability, to address this by regular visits home and by constantly talking to locals who have lived in and loved Emmett their entire lives. But the truth of the matter is that, because I am no longer an Idaho native, there are things I will miss. There are countless stories I doubtless overlooked, or could have told better, if I were living in Emmett. My absence means that my vision, even though it's grown, is still faulty. I cannot truly *know* this place as fully as it ought to be known—unless I move back.

⚹

There, again, is the question. Will I move back?

Many of the factors that prompted me to leave Idaho in the first place are no longer relevant. As an adult, I no longer worry about being seen as my own person and don't bristle at being known by my family—indeed, I'm proud when people back home recognize me as a Howard. My old desire for novelty has changed with time, as I've come to realize that constancy matters as much (if not more) to our world as audacity and daring. I still deeply care about international humanitarian issues, but I've come to realize that poverty, injustice, and violence are local issues too.

One factor has not disappeared. One of the reasons I left Idaho behind was that I felt like an outsider. I was a nerdy bookworm who often did not fit in well within my rural context. When I flew out East for the first time, I was seeking a place where I might find kindred spirits—somewhere I might finally fit in and feel at home.

Now, ten years in Virginia have shaped my character, politics, and philosophies, sometimes in ways that make me fit in even less in the place I left. Idaho is one of the reddest states in the country, politically speaking—but I'm neither Republican nor libertarian these days (as my condemnations of economic concentration and monopolization in this book probably make clear). I find myself grappling with the legacies of injustice in my own state. I am pro-life, but my younger brother has affectionately titled me a "hippie": someone who deeply cares about issues of climate change and ecological stewardship. I sometimes feel as if

[handwritten marginal note: reason for leaving was being an outsider] the people I grew up with back home are hesitant to discuss these things, to grapple with the issues of racial injustice, economic exploitation, or ecological abuse that plague us today. And so I sometimes worry that moving home might result in frustration and loss, rather than in connection and community.

But in these fears, I can recognize the toxic assumptions of a deeply polarized culture, one that influences us all during these fractious and fractured times. This attitude is often eager to stereotype the "other," assuming what people on the other side of the political aisle may or may not believe on a given topic. It is also often hesitant to find common ground—because the political other is often seen as sinister, or as deluded by some outside sinister force. The polarized voices of our world often suggest that alienation and silence are better than difficult conversations or hard-fought battles for empathy.

Even though I know my politics might be strange—even frustrating—to people back in Idaho, avoiding home because of political differences would be wrong. Persuasion happens best through presence, and it's right to seek out ways in which we can love and serve our political enemies. It could be that my political views might serve my homeland. It could also be that, by moving back, my current opinions would be tempered with greater grace and empathy.

More compelling as a reason to stay in Virginia are the roots I've put down over the past decade. The tragic irony in deciding to stick and "live as a perennial" in a new place, I'm learning, is that it makes it very hard to consider ever moving anywhere else—even back to the land where you were born.

Here in Virginia, I've brought Grandma Mom's brown bread to families with new babies (and shared the recipe with others). My husband and I have witnessed weddings and births, attended town meetings, volunteered with local organizations, and built friendships with our neighbors. We've had people visit us in the hospital, support us when we were grieving and tired, and care for our daughters as if for their own children. We have a membership, and it is sweet. We bought a fixer-upper that increasingly feels like a forever home, and I do not want to leave it behind. Although we have not always had the financial freedom to buy all our groceries from local farmers, I have cultivated a vegetable garden for the past five years, and I'm slowly growing in knowledge and seeking to improve our soil with time. We feast on the resulting tomatoes and greens, squash and cucumbers, basil and peppers, and I can feel those roots growing even deeper. We've determined to stick here, and as a result, it feels like our place.

Grandma Mom was a transplant too. After leaving the heartland, she made Emmett better for her presence. And in Grandma Mom, I see a beautiful and compelling example of what life might be like if I were to stay in Virginia. Grandma Mom embraced Idaho—and through her grace and generosity helped many other people put down roots there. She cared deeply about young people in the community, I've heard, and walked with several of them through the most difficult points in their lives. It would be wrong to say she was a "boomer" by moving from North Dakota to Idaho. Everywhere she lived, she chose to be a perennial. Surely, those of us who've moved away from our homelands can aspire to that same grace and passion.

I've found that many people in Virginia crave the sense of community and rootedness that was perhaps a bit more natural and established in my rural context—and I think the rhythms of that world have great applicability here. Over the past couple of years, my husband and I have helped prune a vineyard in winter and make apple butter in the fall, participating in new seasonal traditions that fit this landscape. Just as quilting bees, preserving, corn shucking, and haymaking were common in my homeland, we've started looking for ways to forge strong community bonds through shared labor and love.

Some of my friends recently created a spreadsheet in which we all list projects that need doing, along with dates we are available to work. Each month, one family hosts the rest of us, and we aim to get their project finished. We show up with food and drink, tools and working gloves, eager either to hold babies and watch toddlers or to get our hands dirty working on a needed project. Together we have worked on gardens and patios, sheds and fences. In the process, our friendships have deepened. They no longer exist solely in the realm of "the fun"—the realm of movie and game nights, dinner parties, book clubs, and happy hours. There's something special about actually working with each other: showing our friends and neighbors that we are willing to sweat and toil for them, willing even to get a few splinters or sore muscles for them. It has helped us forge strong memories, share hard-earned expertise, and even teach our children some important lessons about givenness, determination, and diligence. In this little way, I hope I'm living out the legacy of Grandpa Dad, passing down lessons he taught me in a new land.

Moving back to Idaho at this point would require finding and re-forming community: seeking out new kindred spirits and building relationships back up that have waned or grown fragile with the passage of time. That sounds daunting, even frightening at times. But the decision to stick as a transplant also comes with costs— costs that must be acknowledged and reckoned with. It would mean accepting weakening ties to people and places back home. It would also mean accepting my role as bystander amid Idaho's transformation, witnessing its depletion, exploitation, or metamorphosis in coming decades. Without membership and rootedness in my native soil, I have no say in what happens to it next.

It would be horribly hubristic to assume that my own homecoming might make any difference in Idaho's transformation if I *were* to move back. Mere presence would not bring any overwhelming, automatic alterations to my homeland. I would still be a bystander—just a bystander on the front lines, in this instance. To return might simply mean being present for more demise, more loss. Yet I also believe presence can be its own gift: by being present, we can "mourn with those who mourn." We become witnesses to our community's griefs, needs, and joys.

This book has been an exercise in discernment, and thanks to the study and attention it has required, I now know a little better what I might return home to. Because of this project, going home will not be a choice made out of blind nostalgia or homesickness for something that once was. It will be a conscious choice of love,

made to a people and a place that are messy, complicated, broken—
and precious beyond imagining.

With time, I grow more and more certain this homecoming
will happen—even if I am still uncertain how or when it will take
place. My parents are aging, and, like Grandpa Wally, I would
pull up stakes in a heartbeat to be near them—to make sure they
have the support system they need. My husband's family is far
larger than my own, and thus there are plenty of kids and grand-
kids to support his parents in Virginia. Both my parents have
lived in Idaho for their entire lives (as did their parents before
them). We would never expect them to move away, so caring for
them will likely require my homecoming.

In all honesty, that is a prospect that gives me a great deal of
pleasure. My parents have become some of my dearest friends as
I've grown older, and my little girls adore them. Moving to be
near them as they age would have its difficulties, but I truly think
it is something my husband and I would look back on without
regrets. It is a way we can follow in the footsteps of our forebears,
a way to give back to and love those who've given so much to us.

There are still people in my home state who I feel a deep sense
of kinship with—including the members of my parents' Angli-
can church. When my parents began attending this church a few
years back, it made Idaho feel, strangely, more like home than it
did before. Whenever I visit this tiny church, I continue to experience a community that makes me feel like I belong, like I fit in.
This is partially a response to the fact that there are several book-
worms, bakers, and farm lovers in this church—even a couple of
Wendell Berry fans. But it's also the natural response we feel, I

gigi and poppy
Episcople church
in glouchester

think, when we encounter a community that is passionate about caring for its members.

Thanks to the people I love, the prospect of moving back to be near my parents is something I've often dreamed about and looked forward to as I've written this book. I imagine shopping at the farmers' market on Saturday mornings: getting our produce from Waterwheel Gardens or taking my girls to Lance Phillips's orchard in June and August for cherries and peaches. I've dreamed of picking up our beef from Peter and Susan Dill and truly giving back to each of the people in this book I've come to admire and appreciate so deeply. I want to be a part of their membership. It is true that, if we move five or ten years down the road, I have no idea what I will come home to. There's no guarantee these farmers will still be there, or that my idyllic vision of a supportive local food economy will still exist in Emmett or elsewhere. I hope it will. There are strong indications to suggest that it will. But as with all realities in this valley, this is a huge unknown—one I must accept and make my peace with.

For now, at least, my husband's job, our home, and our network are keeping us in Virginia. The puzzle pieces haven't aligned for us to move back—we don't know when we'll be able to sell our fixer-upper, when the perfect jobs might come along that would enable us to move across the country. So we are choosing to stick as transplants in Virginia, cultivating what we have now. And honestly, we're lucky: we love living here and are happy in this place. But I also look forward to going home when the time is right, to hopefully honor the legacy of sticking I've been given.

This book is not meant to suggest that everyone should stick in their community, regardless of its challenges. There are many times and places when it is appropriate—even crucial—to leave. Many Americans have left their homelands to escape trauma, abuse, and racism. We must recognize the fact that policy and prejudice have often forced uprootedness upon populations who would otherwise have cultivated health and diversity in local soil.

Many people also leave their homelands because there is no hope or promise left: the soil has been so degraded over time, there is little to no promise of community, employment, or family belonging left. In *The Need for Roots*, Simone Weil notes that unemployment is itself one of the worst and most dire forms of uprootedness we can experience.[2] Sticking in a place where there are no job opportunities and little promise of change results not in a sticker mentality, but in a passive form of "stuckness" that is debilitating to the soul.

There are many reasons, therefore, to leave a place—even a place we love. But *why* we leave and *what* we cultivate once we've moved to new ground are important questions to consider.

The real danger comes from deciding never to stick at all. In an essay he wrote about his hometown of Sneads, Florida, Timothy Kleiser notes that "physical mobility can paradoxically cause a person to become more place-oriented when their goal is to plant deep roots in their new place. The problem arises—as it did with me—when such mobility becomes *transience*, a state of perpetual movement that makes it impossible to cultivate a strong sense of place."[3]

Many Americans throughout our history have committed themselves to constant transience: They are, as Wallace Stegner put it, "those who pillage and run," who want "to make a killing and end up on Easy Street."[4] They never move with the intention of staying but, instead, seek out the "elsewhere" that always lies beyond: the better job prospects and opportunities that lie on the horizon, just out of reach.

Few such boomers would see themselves as such. Transience is easy to fall into almost passively: the result of our social environment and its pressures, the urgings we receive to "go far," or the constant consumerist messages that push us to climb the economic ladder.

But transience can also be easy—even necessary—in an economy that nurtures near-constant financial uncertainty and anxiety. In his *Quest for Community*, Robert Nisbet suggested that modern economics had fomented instability and a "sense of void" where previous generations experienced "the joy of comradeship and security."[5] If this was true when Nisbet wrote it, in the 1950s, it's surely more applicable to the uncertainty and volatility experienced by American workers today. Many of us may be privileged enough to choose whether we are boomers or stickers, but it would be wrong to ignore the fact that many poor and working-class Americans throughout our history have had transience thrust upon them.

On the other hand, many Americans are far less mobile than they used to be—but they are by no means *more* rooted because of staying in place. A significant population of Americans are now "stuck": unable to leave towns that are dying, with little to no prospect for improvements in social or economic capital. These people bear the brunt both of elites who are boomers by choice, and of working- and middle-class people who are boomers by necessity (but are still, nonetheless, lucky enough to be employed). They are stuck on the bottom rung and unable to do anything about it.

Yet "to be rooted," Weil argues, "is perhaps the most important and least recognized need of the human soul."[6] By neglecting this need and making it difficult for many Americans to be fully rooted in place, it's likely that we have fostered the epidemic of loneliness, anxiety, and drug abuse experienced by many Americans in our own time. We've broken down rural and postindustrial communities and caused many Americans to become stranded in the shells of places left behind.

There was a time when the Drug Enforcement Administration showed up at Grandpa Dad's door, demanding to know what he was growing in the middle of his cornfield. They had seen an aerial view of the field and knew that he had planted something in the middle of it that was shorter than the field corn surrounding it. They suspected this snowy-haired old man might be growing marijuana.

Grandpa Dad assured the concerned agents that he was doing nothing of the sort. He had started a tradition some years back of planting sweet corn—which is about two feet shorter than field corn—in the middle of one of his other cornfields. He didn't want to grow the sweet corn right up to the road's edge because passersby would occasionally stop their cars and help themselves to the crop. (Yes, locals in farm country can tell the difference between the full leaves and tall height of field corn and the shorter, spindlier appearance of sweet corn.)

The sweet corn that Grandpa Dad planted wasn't for him, you see—it was for church folks, neighbors, and family. So Grandpa Dad would plant it a little ways inside the tall rows of field corn, set back just enough from the road to hide it from prying eyes.

The field of hidden sweet corn was Grandpa Dad's first fruits: the crop he grew to give away. It was the corn I shucked with clumsy hands as a little girl and ate all through the cold winter months. It prompted storytelling and feasting, the gathering of the generations to bring in the harvest. That corn planted roots deep inside me: connecting me to Grandpa Dad and to the land that he cared for.

I can imagine Grandpa Dad planting that field in the spring, memorizing poetry and Scripture verses as he worked on his tractor. I'm sure he looked forward to seeing the green tendrils of life erupt from the earth, to the truckloads of corn he would drive to my grandparents' house, to the laughter and music we would all enjoy together. My ancestors were always setting aside a portion of their proceeds to bless the people they loved. Their labor was never just for them: it was a poured-out thing.

Over the past several years, I've learned that the dead can hurt or heal: urge us forward or call us back. This means that the work of the boomers, those who deplete soil and community, can result in long-lasting brokenness. It can take generations to recover from their legacy, to restore what's been depleted. Many of us are still waiting and watching, hoping to see our homelands restored. We are still observing and mourning what has been lost, squandered, or abused.

But stickers, in contrast, can sow blessings in the soil for decades to come. I owe much of the good fruit in my life to my ancestors' lives, labors, and love: to the chain of membership they handed down, the values they passed on, the richness they built in their community. My forebears connected me to much more than the land: They connected me to the dead, who came before me, and to the seasons that surrounded me. They connected me to rhythms of family, community, and virtue that sprung up in this land long before I was born. The portion they set aside resulted in an overflowing abundance of joy and grace.

In his work *Reflections on the Revolution in France*, Edmund Burke suggests that society is not just made up of the living but, rather, serves as an association between the dead, the living, and the unborn.[7] To be indebted is to see oneself as inseparably intertwined with the duties and responsibilities of this membership. We are never entirely solitary or self-determining in this life. Everything we have and are is inescapably tied to those who came before us.

That doesn't mean that we cannot make our own mark on this world, that we cannot forge new paths for ourselves or for our families. But it acknowledges the fact that we are part of a community both dead and alive, and that this reality comes with responsibilities. We Americans delight in seeing ourselves as self-made, as mavericks. Tocqueville was right about us. We don't want to acknowledge what we might owe to the past or to place. But I think Wendell Berry is also right: we should take our membership seriously, considering those dead and alive who have made us who we are, and how we might further their work in the future. The past is never fully past—not for the soil, and not for us.

Modern American life has in many ways weakened our bonds to the past as well as to local customs of indebtedness and generosity. But thanks to people like Grandpa Dad, who planted the seeds of community and sustenance I enjoyed as a child, I still feel a strong sense of obligation to my Idaho family and community. I feel a deep awe and gratitude for the place that nourished me all through my growing-up years. My very identity and personhood would have been impossible if not for the work, love, and investment of my forebears. If they had not stayed in place, I would not have inherited the goodness they cultivated. I never would have seen or known the preciousness of this valley: its hurts and joys, blessings and brokenness.

In my own life, I don't yet know what my crop of first fruits might look like. In many ways, here in Virginia, I'm still finding my footing, still putting down roots. If I move back to Idaho in the future, I will have to doggedly pursue the same goal there—following in the footsteps of Grandpa Dad and Grandma Mom, seeking to build rhythms of grace and givenness. But I want to display this love whether I live as transplant or returner. No matter what, I will choose to be rooted.

Conclusion

There are two different sorts of homesickness. The first is a gentle ache for material things, which I felt soon after I moved to Virginia for college. It's an ache for things that were pleasant and heartwarming as a child—like the smell of pine or the taste of Grandma's pie. These are the things we often associate with nostalgia: the small, material absences or presences that we form rituals around and enjoy, that remind us of the best parts of our childhood. I do not want to negate their importance or sweetness by calling them sentimental, but that is what they are. (And that is not necessarily a bad thing.)

But there's a second form of homesickness that can bubble up in your soul sometimes—often as a reaction to those material items, but going deeper and hurting more. It's an ache for presences past, for the souls that animated and embodied our most beloved memories of home. The ache is often filled with grief and gratitude because our entire idea of home is bound up in their presence, in the way they lived and loved so well. Rather than a gentle ache, it can feel like a raw, burning hurt. In those moments, we feel the absence of the presences that made us who we are, and we long to see them resurrected in our lives. This is why we walk in their footsteps, bake their bread, and tell their stories: to keep them alive, to feel their presences again, to conjure up the comfort they created—even if only for a moment.

"Nostalgia" is derived from the Greek word *nostos*, for "home-coming," and *álgos*, for "pain, ache." I know I'm not alone in experiencing this ache. Many of my friends have also experienced this homesickness and wrestled with it. Perhaps readers of this book have wrestled with it as well. Many of us share those sense memories of our hometowns, of our grandparents, of the people and places who gave us life. Recalling a particular tree, an autumn scent, or the eccentric habit of a deceased loved one can result in a pang of longing.

We choose what to do with this ache. We can ignore it, dismiss it as sentimentality, and push forward with our lives. Or we can pause and consider. What is the pain telling us about what we're missing? What does it tell us about how we might form the future?

Homesickness can become a way to identify the best parts of the past and carry them forward—even as we leave behind things that ought to be reformed or abandoned. In this way, we can prevent nostalgia from turning into a reactionary or bitter habit of thought while still learning from its ache. Homesickness reveals opportunities to respond to love. Perhaps that love will propel us forward to transplant ourselves in better soil, to create healthier rhythms for us and our families.

It is important to recognize that its ache will never be perfectly satisfied by a specific place or community. We should not return home out of an expectation of fulfillment, out of some hope that homecoming will assuage that ache in our hearts. It won't. But perhaps love—a truly clear-eyed, understanding love—will still call us back to what we've left behind and inspire us to invest in communities that raised us, in families that need us, or in landscapes that have been sorely depleted.

Wherever we decide to live, we must learn to stick: choosing to invest ourselves in place, to love our neighbors, to leave our soil a little healthier than it was when we arrived. Every place will be imperfect. Our own efforts at living well in place will be imperfect. But love suggests that we ought to keep trying anyway: to keep sowing seeds of service and generosity in the lands we love.

To choose rootedness, we must acknowledge the fact that, as Simone Weil points out, a desire for profit, unless tempered by other goods and goals, tends to destroy human roots. We have to seek out larger goals than financial fulfillment, than reaching that next rung on the social or economic ladder. We have to consider whether the perfect career or paycheck will offer us the fulfillment or happiness we lack—or whether the cost of transience is, in fact, too high a cost. It is true that providing for ourselves and our families and having solid employment are fundamental considerations. But we must also remember that they are not the only questions or goals worth considering.

If you are conservative, you may have to reckon with the fact that, as Robert Nisbet argues, capitalism is *especially* prone to fostering a vision of the autonomous, rootless individual. Capitalism's "great, impersonal system" sees humans "not as members of society but as individual units of energy and production," Nisbet argues.[1] And while that means we have built a lot of wealth over the course of our history, it also means we have ignored deeper spiritual and communal needs, breaking down social capital along the way.

On the other hand, if you are progressive, you may have to reckon with the fact that individualism and self-actualization are not enough to foster happiness and well-being. The federal government is not enough, on its own, to meet the needs of its citizens. Humans crave membership, within localities and associations—and rather than building a cultural or political environment that would foster this sort of belonging, we've done the opposite. As Christine Emba wrote in 2018 for *The Washington Post*, liberalism "has scoured anything that could hold stable meaning and connection from our modern landscape—culture has been disintegrated, family bonds devalued, connections to the past cut off, an understanding of the common good all but disappeared."[2]

By encouraging social mobility and ignoring the importance of rootedness, both left and right have destroyed the very environment their voters depend upon for happiness and well-being. Many cities and towns have felt the aftereffects. Chapter 10 highlights some changes in federal policy that might help rural communities specifically—but the principles therein, of supporting social networks and associations as well as individuals, could and should also be applied to more urban areas. In their book, *The*

New Localism, Bruce Katz and Jeremy Nowak highlight the efforts of many cities—both in the United States and internationally—to reform their municipalities along such lines.[3] As mentioned earlier in the book, Richard Florida, Patrick Carr, and Maria Kefalas have identified two groups besides the "mobile" and "stuck" who have a beneficial impact on their places: the "rooted," who "have the resources to move but prefer to stay where they are," and the "returners," who build up financial capital elsewhere but then return and invest that capital in their home communities. Both these groups could do (and, indeed, have done) a lot to strengthen their places.

Perhaps we can be the rooted: those who encourage our employees, coworkers, friends, or neighbors to be rooted as well, by seeking to foster health and profit within place (rather than leaving place behind). There are several such stories of community service and investment I have observed within my Idaho community—stories of mom-and-pop businesses that grow, but never leave. Even small efforts aimed at reinvigorating place—volunteering, going to town council meetings, or cleaning up trash on the sidewalk—can serve to encourage rootedness in those around us.

For those of us who have left home behind, perhaps we can offer the hope of a "returner": one of those community members who will be key, in many areas of America, to rebuilding social fabric and economic opportunity. Many places, to quote my brother, need "an IV of cash straight to the bloodstream so they can get on their feet again." Investment of capital at the local level gives these places a little more strength and resilience, a little more hope for the future. Few companies will choose to invest their efforts or resources in struggling towns; thus, their greatest chance for survival may rest with people who have some personal connection to their homelands—people who return home, not out of a desire to be served, but to serve. Perhaps the social or financial capital we've built up in faraway places can provide the jolt of enthusiasm or hope our home communities have needed.

Perhaps we hesitate to make such decisions because we fear "settling." We see going home, or even settling in one place long-term, as failure. We fear such rootedness might reveal that we do not have what it takes—even if we are unsure what it is that we are supposed to have, or where it is we aim to go. We are used to a culture that constantly urges us to "make a mark on the world," to turn ourselves into powerful influencers or world changers of one sort or another. We want to be somebodies and fear becoming nobodies.

Yet as James Rebanks writes in his book *The Shepherd's Life*, "Landscapes like ours were created by and survive through the efforts of nobodies."[4] I still go back to the graveyard whenever I can on my visits home, with flowers under my arm. I plant my feet in a graveyard full of names I do not recognize, along with the few I know and love, and consider what their presence here, their silent membership, represents. Sometimes, I wonder: Where will I be buried? Does it matter what soil my body is planted in, after I'm gone?

Perhaps it's a pointless question. But maybe there's something to be said for the bodies that remain in place, long after they have lived and loved there, staying faithful to the ground they once cared for. Perhaps these graves will testify to something important, long after I or any other visiting relative is gone. These bodies may rest in unremembered graves—but our lives will still be the better for their faithfulness.

I stand here with the dead because I believe they matter. This land matters. And all the roots that sink down deep into this ground, lending strength and life to this soil, will matter long after any of us are gone. No matter how the world determines worth, we must remember and reverence the nobodies who are truly somebodies.

Acknowledgments

T his book has an entire supportive, nourishing community behind it—and I am grateful beyond words for the people whose "constant habit of benevolence" made it possible.

My agent, William Callahan at Inkwell Management Literary Agency, first encouraged me to consider writing a book years ago—long before I thought such a thing could happen—and helped me turn my love of home into a manuscript. Bria Sandford is a wise and steadfast editor who bore with me through the long process of sculpting and bettering this work. The finished product would have been a deficient and half-realized thing without her counsel and guidance. Bless you, Bria. Words cannot express my thanks.

The Emmett farmers, townspeople, and students I talked to while working on this book each impacted this book so deeply. Many of them welcomed me into their home, shared recipes and stories with me, and helped me understand and love this place more than I did before. There are more than I can possibly thank here, but I must offer my gratitude to Peter and Susan Dill, Tracy Walton, Danny Walton, Terry and Ashley Walton, Vaughn and Lisa Jensen, Lucy Lourenco, Lance Phillips, Matt Williams, Brad Little, David Little, Nate Low, FaithAnn Hynek, John Lavergne, Rob and Scott Tyler, Harold and Jackie Williams, Carl Siller, RuthAnn Suyehira, AnaBelen Paul, and Shelby Burlil for giving so generously of their time. Thank you to Deb Marks for sharing the history she wrote about her father, Bob Benson, and thus sharing his incredible life with me and the readers of this book.

There are countless writers (and "writerly friends") whose thoughts and advice have shaped this book. Some helped with content and the vision of the book, while others gave me vital tips on surviving the writing process itself. Thank you to Susannah Black, Jeffrey Bilbro, Jonathan Coppage, Chuck Marohn, Jeremy Beer, Mark Mitchell, Sarah Smarsh, Maria Kefalas, and Jeff Benedict, for offering insights and encouragement along the way. Thank you to Austin Frerick for reading this manuscript and offering his invaluable expertise. My old journalism professor Les Sillars has been a wonderful source of wisdom and advice over the years, and was kind enough to read an early manuscript and offer his thoughts. Daniel McCarthy, Jim Antle, and Lewis McCrary commissioned and polished many essays and writings that led to this book. Thank you to Jake Meador and the entire Mere Orthodoxy team for encouraging and supporting me as I worked on this book. Thank you to Leah Libresco and Catherine Addington, for praying for me when I needed it.

My Grandpa Wally's cousin Janet Isaacson loaned me several rare books, family letters, genealogies, and photographs that were invaluable as I sought to write the sections of this book that consider Emmett's history and my own family history. I cannot thank her enough for her tenacious work in chronicling the Howards' stories, and for sharing her findings so generously with me.

Thank you to my core team of confidants and advisers: Hannah, Yetta, Christine, Beth, Laura, Sarah, Chelsea, and Courtney. Each of you contributed to this work through your prayers, humor, and kindness. Thank you for providing space for me to write via free babysitting, lunch and coffee, a quiet working space, and more. Thank you to Sarah and her husband, Nathan, for reading multiple iterations of these chapters with such enthusiasm.

Thank you to Wendell Berry, whose books planted the seeds for this work over a decade ago, and whose letters have served as a constant source of wisdom and inspiration. It was Mr. Berry who first urged me to tell the story of my family. I have been blessed countless times by his guidance and counsel.

Thank you to my sweet siblings-in-law, for your constant encouragement and love as I worked through this writing process. I could not ask for a sweeter, more supportive family. Mark and Becky, thank you for watching my girls, reading chapters, and checking in on me as I worked through this long process!

Thank you to my sweet, wonderful siblings—Katie, James, and Johnny—for your encouragement, love, and care. I couldn't have done this without you. In particular, I must thank James for reading the manuscript, for helping me track down important data, and for the countless phone and email conversations regarding place and economics that ended up getting quoted or referenced in this book.

Grandpa Wally, you once suggested that perhaps I could write a book about you someday. Now I've done it, and I hope you like it. Thank you for all the stories and traditions that you and Grandma Elaine wove into the fabric of my life. Thank you for being willing to share so much of your own story with me over the past few years, for giving of your time and memories in order to make this book come alive.

My superhero parents babysat my little girls and loaned me their car on countless trips home so that I could drive around interviewing people and sit in coffee shops scribbling notes. Their counsel and thoughts improved and shaped this book. Thank you to my wonderful mother for reminding me that "we have this treasure in jars of clay." Thank you to my wise and selfless father, for fact-checking this manuscript with an expert regional knowledge that is itself the result of a lifetime of sticking and loving.

Several years ago, I sat outside a restaurant with my husband and told him I didn't think I could write a book. I didn't think I would have time. I didn't think my ideas or my writing were good enough. He believed in me and urged me to keep going. He provided time, inspiration, and support every step of the way. He is this book's first editor, an astute adviser, and a constant source of encouragement. He reminds me of my Grandpa Dad, and much of this book is inspired by his character and virtue. I will always be grateful for you, Eli.

Notes

INTRODUCTION

1. Kevin D. Williamson, "If Your Town Is Failing, Just Go," *National Review*, October 6, 2015, https://www.nationalreview.com/2015/10/mobility-globaliza tion-poverty-solution/.

CHAPTER 1

1. "Fruitland, Idaho, United States: % Staying in Same Commuting Zone as Adults," Opportunity Atlas, accessed August 10, 2020, https://www.opportunity atlas.org/.
2. "Emmett, Idaho, United States: % Staying in Same Commuting Zone as Adults," Opportunity Atlas, accessed August 10, 2020, https://www.opportunity atlas.org/.
3. "McCall, Idaho, United States: % Staying in Same Commuting Zone as Adults," Opportunity Atlas, accessed August 10, 2020, https://www.opportunity atlas.org/.
4. "Boise Metro Area: Workforce Trends," Idaho Department of Labor, last modified June 2020, https://lmi.idaho.gov/Portals/0/2020/WorkforceTrends /BoiseMSAprofile.pdf.
5. "Emmett, Idaho, United States."
6. According to U.S. Census Bureau data, the median age in Gem County has steadily moved upward for the past several years, from age 41.7 to age 45.1 between 2010 and 2018 alone. The number of youths under eighteen has dropped from 26.2 percent of the population to 23.4 percent of the population in that same time frame. Sources: "2018: ACS 5-Year Estimates Subject Tables, Age and Sex," and "2010: ACS 5-Year Estimates Subject Tables, Age and Sex," https://data.census.gov/cedsci/.
7. Patrick J. Carr and Maria J. Kefalas, *Hollowing Out the Middle: The Rural Brain Drain and What It Means for America* (Boston: Beacon Press, 2009), 1.
8. Carr and Kefalas, *Hollowing Out the Middle*, 2.

CHAPTER 2

1. "Soil Survey: Gem County Area Idaho," U.S. Department of Agriculture Soil Conservation Service, September 1965, 183–84, https://www.blogs.nrcs .usda.gov/Internet/FSE_MANUSCRIPTS/idaho/gemID1965/gemID 1965.pdf.

2. Hiram Taylor French, *History of Idaho: A Narrative Account of Its Historical Progress, Its People and Principal Interests* (Chicago and New York: Lewis Publishing Company, 1914), 284.

3. Department of Commerce and Labor Bureau of the Census, "Statistics for Idaho: Containing Statistics of Population, Agriculture, Manufactures, and Mining for the State, Counties, Cities, and Other Divisions," 1910, https:// www2.census.gov/library/publications/decennial/1910/abstract/supplement -id.pdf.

4. John W. Heaton, *The Shoshone-Bannocks: Culture and Commerce at Fort Hall, 1870–1940* (Lawrence: University Press of Kansas, 2005), 24.

5. E. B. Bentley, Bill Bonnischen, John C. Freemuth, Bill Hackett, Glenn Oakley, F. Ross Peterson, Mark G. Plew, Todd Shallatt, and Steve Stuebner, "SNAKE: The Plain and Its People," Boise State University ScholarWorks, 1994, 75, https://scholarworks.boisestate.edu/cgi/viewcontent.cgi?article=1371&context =fac_books.

6. Ruth B. Lyon, *The Village That Grew* (Boise: Lithocraft, 1991), 1.

7. Lyon, *The Village That Grew*, 23.

8. Ralph H. Hess, "The Beginnings of Irrigation in the United States," *Journal of Political Economy* 20, no. 8 (October 1912): 812, https://www.journals.uchicago .edu/doi/pdf/10.1086/252096.

9. "Inactive and Abandoned Mines," Idaho Geological Survey, accessed August 10, 2020, https://www.idahogeology.org/inactive-mines.

10. Lyon, *The Village That Grew*, 4.

11. Lyon, 16.

12. Lyon, 45–60.

13. "Pickett's Corral," Idaho State Historical Society Reference Series 253, March 1972, https://history.idaho.gov/wp-content/uploads/0253_Pickets-Corral.pdf.

14. Lyon, *The Village That Grew*, 78, 104, and 157.

15. Wallace Stegner, *Where the Bluebird Sings to the Lemonade Springs: Living and Writing in the West* (New York: Random House, 2002), xxvii.

16. Stegner, *Where the Bluebird Sings to the Lemonade Springs*, xxii.

17. Leonard J. Arrington, *History of Idaho* (Moscow: University of Idaho Press, 1994), 287, https://law.resource.org/pub/us/code/id/idaho.history.2.pdf.

18. Laurie Mercier, "Confronting Race and Creating Community: Idaho's Ethnic History," in *Idaho's Place: A New History of the Gem State*, ed. Adam M. Sowards (Seattle: University of Washington Press, 2014), 175–76.

19. Robert T. Hayashi, *Haunted by Waters: A Journey Through Race and Place in the American West* (Iowa City: University of Iowa Press, 2007), 29.

20. Hayashi, *Haunted by Waters*, 30.

21. Bentley et al., "SNAKE," 128.

22. "Hydraulic Mining Techniques, California, 1870s," U.S. Geological Survey, accessed August 10, 2020, https://www.usgs.gov/media/images/hydraulic -mining-techniques-california-1870s.

23. Leon F. Neuenschwander, James W. Byler, Alan E. Harvey, Geral I. McDonald, Denise S. Ortiz, Harold L. Osborne, Gerry C. Snyder, and Arthur Zack, "White Pine in the American West: A Vanishing Species—Can We Save It?" U.S. Department of Agriculture Forest Service, August 1999, https://www .fs.fed.us/rm/pubs/rmrs_gtr035.pdf.

24. Lyon, *The Village That Grew*, 80.

25. "Japanese Americans in the Columbia River Basin," Washington State University, accessed August 10, 2020, https://content.libraries.wsu.edu/digital /collection/cchm/custom/ja-overview.

26. Hayashi, *Haunted by Waters*, 62.

27. Alice Y. Hashitani Nashitani, "Henry Katsuji and Takako Hashitani Retrospective," Washington State University Vancouver Library, 1, https://content .libraries.wsu.edu/digital/collection/imls_3/id/213.

28. Nashitani, "Henry Katsuji and Takako Hashitani Retrospective," 1.

29. Nashitani, 1–2.

30. "Alien Land Laws," Densho Encyclopedia, accessed August 10, 2020, https:// encyclopedia.densho.org/Alien_land_laws/.

31. Eric Walz, *Nikkei in the Interior West: Japanese Immigration and Community Building, 1882–1945* (Tucson: University of Arizona Press, 2012), 110.

32. Andrew Jenson, *Encyclopedic History of the Church of Jesus Christ of Latter-day Saints* (Salt Lake City: Deseret News, 1941), 85, https://contentdm.lib.byu .edu/digital/collection/BYUIBooks/id/2600.

33. "Mormons by State," Pew Research Center, accessed August 10, 2020, https:// www.pewforum.org/religious-landscape-study/religious-tradition/mormon/.

34. "Soil Survey: Gem County Area Idaho," U.S. Department of Agriculture Soil Conservation Service, 184.

35. Lyon, *The Village That Grew*, 199.

36. Lyon, 200–203.

37. Lyon, 239.

38. Lyon, 239.

39. Lyon, 237.

40. Lyon, 241.

41. Department of Commerce and Labor Bureau of the Census, "Statistics for Idaho," 608.

42. Lyon, *The Village That Grew*, 241–42.

43. Lyon, 242.

44. Lyon, 81.

45. French, *History of Idaho*, 277.

46. "The New Railroad Reaches Emmett," *Emmett Index*, April 3, 1902, http://www.gemcountymuseum.org/history-railroad.html.

47. Louise Shadduck, *Andy Little: Idaho Sheep King* (Caldwell, ID: Caxton Printers, 1990), 2.

48. Shadduck, *Andy Little*, 56.

49. Shadduck, 71.

50. Lyon, *The Village That Grew*, 133.

51. Lyon, 105.

52. Shadduck, *Andy Little*, 71.

53. Shadduck, 80.

54. "U.S. Basque Population," North American Basque Organizations, accessed August 10, 2020, https://nabasque.eus/us_basque_population.html.

55. Shadduck, *Andy Little*, 110.

CHAPTER 3

1. Leonard J. Arrington, "Idaho and the Great Depression," *Idaho Yesterdays* XIII (Summer 1969): 2, https://digitalatlas.cose.isu.edu/geog/demgrphc/depressn.pdf.

2. Arrington, "Idaho and the Great Depression," 3.

3. Syd Albright, "Idaho Rides Out the Great Depression: It Wasn't Easy," *Coeur d'Alene/Post Falls Press*, October 27, 2013.

4. Arrington, "Idaho and the Great Depression," 3–4.

5. Interviews with my grandfather on this subject were supplemented by a newspaper clip he provided: Patricia R. McCoy, "Frugal Lessons of 1930s Serve 66-Year Farm Career," *Capital Press*, date unknown.

CHAPTER 4

1. John Ikerd, "The Economic Colonization of Rural America," *Daily Yonder*, February 28, 2018, https://www.dailyyonder.com/economic-colonization-rural-america/2018/02/28/.

2. Sarah Smarsh, *Heartland: A Memoir of Working Hard and Being Broke in the Richest Country on Earth* (New York: Scribner, 2018), 98.

3. U.S. Department of the Interior Bureau of Reclamation, "Canal Operation and Maintenance: Vegetation," November 2017, https://www.usbr.gov/asset management/docs/Canal_Vegetation.pdf.

4. Ronald Jager, *The Fate of Family Farming: Variations on an American Idea* (Lebanon, NH: University Press of New England, 2004), 27.

5. Alexis de Tocqueville, *Democracy in America* (Chicago: University of Chicago Press, 2000), 527.

6. Tocqueville, *Democracy in America*, 527.

7. Tocqueville, 529.

8. Wendell Berry, "Renewing Husbandry," *Orion Magazine*, accessed August 14, 2020, https://orionmagazine.org/article/renewing-husbandry/.

9. Lara Bryant, "Lessons of the Dust Bowl," National Wildlife Federation, October 19, 2012, https://blog.nwf.org/2012/10/lessons-of-the-dust-bowl/.

10. Timothy Egan, *The Worst Hard Time: The Untold Story of Those Who Survived the Great American Dust Bowl* (New York: Mariner Books, 2006), 24.

11. John Opie, *The Law of the Land: Two Hundred Years of American Farmland Policy* (Lincoln: University of Nebraska Press, 1994), 99.

12. Mark Fiege, *Irrigated Eden: The Making of an Agricultural Landscape in the American West* (Seattle: University of Washington Press, 2000), 17.

13. Wallace Stegner, *Beyond the Hundredth Meridian: John Wesley Powell and the Second Opening of the West* (New York: Penguin Books, 1992), 228.

14. Carla R. Standley, *The First 100 Years: History of Emmett Irrigation District 1910–2010* (printed by the author), 14.

15. Ruth B. Lyon, *The Village That Grew* (Boise: Lithocraft, 1991), 214.

16. Opie, *The Law of the Land*, 99.

17. Egan, *The Worst Hard Time*, 43.

18. Egan, 43.

19. Louise Shadduck, *Andy Little: Idaho Sheep King* (Caldwell, ID: Caxton Printers, 1990), 228–29.

20. "About Us," Idaho Soil and Water Conservation Commission, accessed August 14, 2020, https://swc.idaho.gov/about-us/.

21. Carl R. O'Connor, "Disaster in the Heartland: The American Dust Bowl," Master's thesis, College at Brockport: State University of New York, December 2009, 9, https://digitalcommons.brockport.edu/ehd_theses/244/

22. R. Douglas Hurt, *Problems of Plenty: The American Farmers in the 20th Century* (Chicago: Ivan R. Dee, 2003), 13.

23. Hurt, *Problems of Plenty*, 12.

24. Hurt, 44.

25. Hurt, 13.

26. Jerome M. Stam and Bruce L. Dixon, *Farmer Bankruptcies and Exits in the United States, 1899–2002*, U.S. Department of Agriculture Economic Research Service, March 2004, 11, https://www.ers.usda.gov/webdocs/publications/42532/17750_aib788_1_.pdf?v=.

27. Hurt, *Problems of Plenty*, 98.

28. Jonathan Coppess, *The Fault Lines of Farm Policy: A Legislative and Political History of the Farm Bill* (Lincoln: University of Nebraska Press, 2018), 170.

29. Egan, *The Worst Hard Time*, 311.

30. Paul Johnstone, "Old Ideals versus New Ideas in Farm Life," in *Farmers in a Changing World: The Yearbook of Agriculture 1940* (Washington, DC: U.S. Government Printing Office, 1940), 140.

31. Coppess, *The Fault Lines of Farm Policy*, 139.

32. Marty Strange, *Family Farming: A New Economic Vision* (Lincoln: University of Nebraska Press, 1988), 18.

33. Strange, *Family Farming*, 19.

34. Stephanie Anderson, *One Size Fits None: A Farm Girl's Search for the Promise of Regenerative Agriculture* (Lincoln: University of Nebraska Press, 2019), 20.

35. Strange, *Family Farming*, 23.

36. Strange, 15.

37. Anderson, *One Size Fits None*, 192–93.

38. American Society of Agronomy, "Research Digs into Root Interactions," *AgriView*, June 17, 2018, https://www.agupdate.com/agriview/news/crop/research -digs-into-root-interactions/article_1b7ae8bd-b2fe-5ac5-96e2-2edb470b3d09 .html.

39. Regina L. Wilpiszeski, Jayde A. Aufrecht, Scott T. Retterer, Matthew B. Sullivan, David E. Graham, Eric M. Pierce, Olivier D. Zablocki, Anthony V. Palumbo, Dwayne A. Elias, "Soil Aggregate Microbial Communities: Towards Understanding Microbiome Interactions at Biologically Relevant Scales," *Applied and Environmental Microbiology* 85, no. 14 (July 2019), https://aem.asm .org/content/aem/85/14/e00324-19.full.pdf.

40. Jessica Murri, "How Healthy Is Idaho's Soil?," *Boise Weekly*, March 12, 2015, https://www.boiseweekly.com/boise/how-healthy-is-idahos-soil /Content?oid=3430628.

41. Mark Bittman, "Now This Is Natural Food," *New York Times*, October 22, 2013, https://www.nytimes.com/2013/10/23/opinion/bittman-now-this-is-natural -food.html.

42. Fred Bahnson, "Farmed Out: Wes Jackson on the Need to Reinvent Agriculture," *The Sun*, October 2010, https://www.thesunmagazine.org/issues/418 /farmed-out.

43. Bahnson, "Farmed Out."

44. Patrick Marley, "Trump Ag Secretary Sonny Perdue Says Dairy Farms Will Survive, but May Have to Get Bigger," *Milwaukee Journal Sentinel*, October 1, 2019, https://www.jsonline.com/story/news/politics/2019/10/01/trump-ag -secretary-says-dairy-farms-have-get-bigger-survive/3829320002/.

45. Ikerd, "The Economic Colonization of Rural America."

46. U.S. Joint Economic Committee–Republicans, "Losing Our Minds: Brain Drain Across the United States," Social Capital Project, April 2019, https:// www.jec.senate.gov/public/index.cfm/republicans/2019/4/losing-our-minds -brain-drain-across-the-united-states.

47. Sean Illing, "A Princeton Sociologist Spent 8 Years Asking Rural Americans Why They're So Pissed Off," *Vox*, June 30, 2018, https://www.vox.com/2018/3/13/17053886/trump-rural-america-populism-racial-resentment.

48. Tom Philpott, "Reviving a Much-Cited, Little-Read Sustainable-Ag Masterpiece," *Grist*, March 2, 2007, https://grist.org/article/soil/.

CHAPTER 5

1. Ben Falk, "Build Healthy Soil Through Regenerative Grazing," *Mother Earth News*, September 2014, https://www.motherearthnews.com/homesteading-and-livestock/sustainable-farming/regenerative-grazing-ze0z1409zhur.

2. "Our Farm and Thinking," Saint John's Organic Farm, accessed August 14, 2010, https://www.saintjohnsorganicfarm.com/what-we-do.

3. Heather Smith Thomas, "Ranchers Sing the Praises of Mob Grazing of Cattle," *BeefMagazine*, February 28, 2012, https://www.beefmagazine.com/pasture-range/ranchers-sing-praises-mob-grazing-cattle.

4. Chris G. Henry and L. Jason Krutz, "Surge Irrigation Information," University of Arkansas Division of Agriculture Research & Extension, May 1, 2017, https://www.uaex.edu/environment-nature/water/Surge%20Irrigation%20Factsheet%202017.pdf.

5. Ron Nichols, "Surge Irrigation Saves Money, Water," *FarmProgress*, May 23, 2003, https://www.farmprogress.com/surge-irrigation-saves-money-water.

6. "Water Q&A: Which States Irrigated the Most?" U.S. Geological Survey, accessed August 14, 2020, https://www.usgs.gov/special-topic/water-science-school/science/water-qa-which-states-use-most-water?qt-science_center_objects=0#qt-science_center_objects.

7. Ed Yong, "What America Lost When It Lost the Bison," *The Atlantic*, November 18, 2019, https://www.theatlantic.com/science/archive/2019/11/how-bison-create-spring/602176/.

8. Stephanie Anderson, *One Size Fits None: A Farm Girl's Search for the Promise of Regenerative Agriculture* (Lincoln: University of Nebraska Press, 2019), 82.

9. Anderson, *One Size Fits None*, 82.

10. Emily Atkin, "You Will Have to Make Sacrifices to Save the Planet," *The New Republic*, June 3, 2019, https://newrepublic.com/article/154036/will-make-sacrifices-save-planet.

CHAPTER 6

1. Cindy Snyder, "Corn Planting in Full Swing in Southern Idaho," MagicValley.com, May 17, 2011, https://magicvalley.com/business/local/corn-planting-in-full-swing-in-southern-idaho/article_843a93dd-1a62-5c84-8849-1d98bc15a3cd.html.

2. Hunter Aten, "The Production of Seed Corn: Planting Through Harvest," Western Illinois University School of Agriculture, https://wiuag.wordpress .com/2016/11/19/the-production-of-seed-corn-planting-through-harvest/.

3. Lee Panella, Stephen R. Kaffka, Robert T. Lewellen, J. Mitchell McGrath, Mike S. Metzger, and Carl A. Strausbaugh, "Sugarbeet," *Yield Gains in Major U.S. Field Crops*, CSSA Special Publication 33, May 12, 2004, https://naldc.nal .usda.gov/download/60057/PDF.

4. Tom Philpott, "Book Review: Why the 'Green Revolution' Was Not So Green After All," *Mother Jones*, August 5, 2011, https://www.motherjones.com/food /2011/08/green-revolution-cullather/.

5. Kristina Hubbard, "Out of Hand: Farmers Face the Consequences of a Con-solidated Seed Industry," Farmer to Farmer Campaign on Genetic Engineering, December 2009, 12, http://www.farmertofarmercampaign.com/Out%20of%20 Hand.FullReport.pdf.

6. Hubbard, "Out of Hand," 4.

7. "Producing Sugarbeet Seed," American Crystal Sugar Company, accessed August 14, 2020, https://www.crystalsugar.com/sugarbeet-agronomy/crystal -beet-seed/producing-sugarbeet-seed/.

8. Brian Scott, "What's in a Monsanto Contract?" *The Farmer's Life*, December 6, 2016, https://thefarmerslife.com/whats-in-a-monsanto-contract/.

9. Hubbard, "Out of Hand," 22.

10. Paul Harris, "Monsanto Sued Small Farmers to Protect Seed Patents, Re-port Says," *The Guardian*, February 12, 2013, https://www.theguardian.com /environment/2013/feb/12/monsanto-sues-farmers-seed-patents.

11. Philip H. Howard, "Global Seed Industry Changes Since 2013," PhilHoward.net, December 31, 2018, https://philhoward.net/2018/12/31/global-seed-industry -changes-since-2013/.

12. Claire Kelloway, "How to Close the Democrats' Rural Gap," *Washington Monthly*, January/February/March 2019, https://washingtonmonthly.com /magazine/january-february-march-2019/how-to-close-the-democrats -rural-gap/.

13. *Pacific Standard* staff, "Consolidation and Mergers Are Eating Our Farm and Food Economy," *Pacific Standard*, June 14, 2017, https://psmag.com/news /consolidation-and-mergers-are-eating-our-farm-and-food-economy.

14. Jeff Desjardins, "The Illusion of Choice in Consumer Brands," *Visual Capitalist*, July 21, 2016, https://www.visualcapitalist.com/illusion-of-choice-consumer -brands/.

15. Austin Frerick, "To Revive Rural America, We Must Fix Our Broken Food System," *The American Conservative*, February 27, 2019, https://www.the americanconservative.com/articles/to-revive-rural-america-we-must-fix-our -broken-food-system/.

16. Patty Bowen, "Dairy Industry Continues to Thrive in Idaho While Dwindling in Meridian," *Idaho Press-Tribune*, June 22, 2018, https://www.idahpress.com/meridian/news/dairy-industry-continues-to-thrive-in-idaho-while-dwindling-in/article_ba1e4e6c-05c3-57bc-8772-0cd638a070cb.html.

17. Ben Eborn, "2018 Proved Tough for Idaho Farms, as Revenue Declined and Dairies Closed Down," *Idaho Statesman*, January 6, 2019, https://www.idahostatesman.com/article224000530.html.

18. Jodi Gralnick and Contessa Brewer, "Dairy Farmers Are Struggling as They Are Squeezed Out of a Changing Milk Market," CNBC, June 1, 2018, https://www.cnbc.com/2018/06/01/dairy-farmers-are-struggling-as-they-are-squeezed-out-of-a-changing-milk-market.html.

19. Rick Barrett, "Dairy Farmers Are in Crisis—and It Could Change Wisconsin Forever," *Milwaukee Journal Sentinel*, February 21, 2019, https://www.jsonline.com/in-depth/news/special-reports/dairy-crisis/2019/02/21/wisconsin-dairy-farms-failing-milk-prices-fall/2540796002/.

20. Paul Heintz, "Selling the Herd: A Milk Price Crisis Is Devastating Vermont's Dairy Farms," *Seven Days*, April 11, 2018, https://www.sevendaysvt.com/vermont/selling-the-herd-a-milk-price-crisis-is-devastating-vermonts-dairy-farms/Content?oid=14631009.

21. Bowen, "Dairy Industry Continues to Thrive in Idaho While Dwindling in Meridian."

22. Bowen.

23. Zach Kyle, "Why Idaho's Family Farms Keep Getting Bigger," *Idaho Statesman*, July 19, 2016, https://www.idahostatesman.com/news/business/business-insider/article90708167.html.

24. Richard Manning, "Idaho's Sewer System Is the Snake River," *High Country News*, August 11, 2014, https://www.hcn.org/issues/46.13/idahos-sewer-system-is-the-snake-river.

25. Associated Press, "2018 Proved Tough for Idaho Farms, as Revenue Declined and Dairies Closed Down," *Idaho Statesman*, January 6, 2019, https://www.idahostatesman.com/article224000530.html.

26. Manning, "Idaho's Sewer System Is the Snake River."

27. Local 8 News Team, "Is a Dairy Crisis Looming in Idaho?" Local News 8, January 25, 2018, https://localnews8.com/news/2018/01/25/is-a-dairy-crisis-looming-in-idaho/.

28. Emily Jones, "Rep. Simpson, Six Others Introduce Immigration Bill," *Idaho Mountain Express*, November 22, 2019, https://www.mtexpress.com/news/business/rep-simpson-six-others-introduce-immigration-bill/article_4f5570c6-0ca9-11ea-9f6e-77933a023dae.html.

29. Times Editorial Board, "Farmworkers Are Treated Unfairly in California. Sacramento Has a Chance to Right That Wrong," *Los Angeles Times*, May 25, 2016,

https://www.latimes.com/opinion/editorials/la-ed--farm-worker-overtime
-20160524-snap-story.html.

30. "Farmworker Health Factsheet," National Center for Farmworker Health,
September 2012, http://www.ncfh.org/uploads/3/8/6/8/38685499/fs-migrant
_demographics.pdf.

31. Phil McCausland, "Best Advice to U.S. Dairy Farmers? 'Sell Out as Fast as
You Can,'" NBC News, June 29, 2018, https://www.nbcnews.com/news/us
-news/best-advice-u-s-dairy-farmers-sell-out-fast-you-n887941.

32. Phil McCausland, "Best Advice to U.S. Dairy Farmers?"

CHAPTER 7

1. Chris Bennett, "It's a Teff Little Grain," *AgProfessional*, November 1, 2018,
https://www.agprofessional.com/article/its-teff-little-grain.

2. "About Us," Teff Company, accessed August 14, 2020, https://teffco.com
/about-us/.

3. Bennett, "It's a Teff Little Grain."

4. "2017 Census of Agriculture County Profile: Gem County Idaho," U.S. Department of Agriculture National Agricultural Statistics Service, 2017, https://
www.nass.usda.gov/Publications/AgCensus/2017/Online_Resources
/County_Profiles/Idaho/cp16045.pdf.

5. "2017 Census of Agriculture Highlights: Farm Producers," U.S. Department
of Agriculture National Agricultural Statistics Service, ACH17-2, April 2019,
https://www.nass.usda.gov/Publications/Highlights/2019/2017Census
_Farm_Producers.pdf.

6. "Feds Pay $24 Million to Idaho Ag Operations Over Trade War," Associ-
ated Press, July 29, 2019, https://apnews.com/839595ca78d74efabb64cd7be4
c5125c.

7. Patrick J. Carr and Maria J. Kefalas, *Hollowing Out the Middle: The Rural Brain
Drain and What It Means for America* (Boston: Beacon Press, 2009), 9.

8. Ezra Klein and Susannah Locke, "40 Maps That Explain Food in America,"
Vox, June 9, 2014, https://www.vox.com/a/explain-food-america.

9. "A Closer Look at the 2018 Farm Bill: Farming Opportunities Training and
Outreach Program," National Sustainable Agriculture Coalition, February 19,
2019, https://sustainableagriculture.net/blog/closer-look-foto-2018-farmbill/.

10. "Loans for Beginning Farmers and Ranchers," AgCredit, accessed August 14,
2020, https://www.agcredit.net/loans/beginning-farmer-loans/fsa-loans.

11. "Commodity Subsidies in the United States Totaled $223.5 Billion from 1995–
2019," Environmental Working Group, August 14, 2020, https://farm.ewg.org
/progdetail.php?fips=00000&progcode=totalfarm&page=conc&regionname
=theUnitedStates.

12. Andrew Soergel, "Family Farms Pushed to Get Big or Go Bust," *U.S. News & World Report*, August 4, 2018, https://www.usnews.com/news/best-states/articles/2018-04-04/family-farms-pushed-to-get-big-or-go-bust.

13. Joel Salatin, *Fields of Farmers: Interning, Mentoring, Partnering, Germinating* (Polyface, 2013), 8–9.

14. Salatin, *Fields of Farmers*, xvii.

15. Richard Florida, "Why Some Americans Won't Move, Even for a Higher Salary," Nextgov, June 6, 2019, https://www.nextgov.com/cio-briefing/2019/06/why-some-americans-wont-move-even-higher-salary/157494/.

16. Carr and Kefalas, *Hollowing Out the Middle*, 19–26.

17. Carr and Kefalas, 139.

18. Christopher Lasch, *The Revolt of the Elites and the Betrayal of Democracy* (New York: W. W. Norton & Company, 1996), 5.

19. Alvin Chang, "Those Who Leave Home, and Those Who Stay," *Vox*, July 25, 2018, https://www.vox.com/policy-and-politics/2017/6/15/15757708/hometown-stay-leave.

20. Wendell Berry, *Nathan Coulter* (Berkeley, CA: Counterpoint, 2008), 7.

21. Berry, *Nathan Coulter*, 7.

22. Sarah Smarsh, *Heartland: A Memoir of Working Hard and Being Broke in the Richest Country on Earth* (New York: Scribner, 2018), 247.

CHAPTER 8

1. Ruth B. Lyon, *The Village That Grew* (Boise: Lithocraft), 245.

2. Lyon, *The Village That Grew*, 249.

3. "Quick Stats," U.S. Department of Agriculture National Agricultural Statistics Service, 2017, https://quickstats.nass.usda.gov/data/printable/A555681E-DB19-3083-9238-57FB05F737B2.

4. "Rural Hunger and Access to Healthy Food," Rural Health Information Hub, accessed August 15, 2020, https://www.ruralhealthinfo.org/topics/food-and-hunger.

5. Chuck Marohn, "The Emptying Out of Rural Kansas: An Interview with Corie Brown," Strong Towns, August 30, 2018, https://www.strongtowns.org/journal/2018/8/30/the-emptying-out-of-rural-kansas.

6. "Benefits of Compost," U.S. Composting Council, accessed August 15, 2020, https://www.compostingcouncil.org/page/CompostBenefits.

7. Jessica Fortis, "Waterwheel Gardens at the Capital City Public Market," *Totally Boise*, November 20, 2018, https://totallyboise.com/Local-Stories/ArticleID/38/Waterwheel-Gardens-at-the-Capital-City-Public-Market.

8. Ezra Klein and Susannah Locke, "40 Maps That Explain Food in America," *Vox*, June 9, 2014, https://www.vox.com/a/explain-food-america.

9. "Idaho Food Stamp Program," Center on Budget and Policy Priorities, March 16, 2020, https://www.cbpp.org/sites/default/files/atoms/files/snap_factsheet _idaho.pdf.

10. "Food Insecurity in the United States," Feeding America *Map the Meal Gap*, accessed August 15, 2020, https://map.feedingamerica.org.

11. "Food Security in the U.S.: Key Statistics and Graphics," U.S. Department of Agriculture Economic Research Service, accessed August 15, 2020, https:// www.ers.usda.gov/topics/food-nutrition-assistance/food-security-in-the-us /key-statistics-graphics.aspx#foodsecure.

12. Phaedra Hise, "Why Does a Strawberry Grown Down the Road Cost More Than One Grown in California?" *The Washington Post*, June 21, 2016, https:// www.washingtonpost.com/lifestyle/food/why-local-food-costs-more -a-strawberry-case-study/2016/06/20/c7177c56-331f-11e6-8ff7-7b6c1998b7a0 _story.html.

13. Brad Plumer, "Map: Here's How Much Each Country Spends on Food," *Vox*, August 19, 2015, https://www.vox.com/2014/7/6/5874499/map-heres-how-much -every-country-spends-on-food.

14. "Food Prices and Spending," U.S. Department of Agriculture Economic Re-search Service, November 29, 2018, https://www.ers.usda.gov/data-products /ag-and-food-statistics-charting-the-essentials/food-prices-and-spending/.

15. Nigel Key, "Farms That Sell Directly to Consumers May Stay in Business Longer," U.S. Department of Agriculture Economic Research Service, April 28, 2016, https://www.usda.gov/media/blog/2016/04/28/farms-sell-directly -consumers-may-stay-business-longer.

16. "2012 Census of Agriculture Highlights: Direct Farm Sales of Food," U.S. Department of Agriculture National Agricultural Statistics Service, ACH 12-35, December 2016, https://www.nass.usda.gov/Publications/Highlights/2016 /LocalFoodsMarketingPractices_Highlights.pdf.

17. Arthur Delaney, "New Farm Bill Won't Save Small Farmers," *The Huffington Post*, December 12, 2018, https://www.huffingtonpost.com/entry/farm-bill -small-farmers_us_5c116676e4b0449012f64078.

18. "Peasant and Family Farm-Based Sustainable Agriculture Can Feed the World," La Vía Campesina, September 2010, https://viacampesina.org/en/wp-content /uploads/sites/2/2010/04/Small-Farmere-Feed-the-World.compressed.pdf.

19. Sarah Chodosh, "We Spend Most of the Year Eating Really, Really Old Apples. Why Do They Taste So Good?" *Popular Science*, December 1, 2017, https://www .popsci.com/winter-apple-old-ripening/.

20. Alice Dubin and Chris Serico, "That Apple You Just Bought Might Be a Year Old—but Does It Matter?" *TODAY*, October 13, 2014, https://www.today.com /food/apple-you-just-bought-might-be-year-old-does-it-2D80207170.

CHAPTER 9

1. Wallace Stegner, *Angle of Repose* (New York: Vintage Books, 2000), 417.

2. Carissa Wolf, "Development Takes a Bite Out of Farmland," *Edible Idaho*, June 28, 2018, http://edibleidaho.ediblecommunities.com/food-thought/development-takes-bite-out-farmland.

3. "Nevada and Idaho Are the Nation's Fastest-Growing States," U.S. Census Bureau, December 19, 2018, https://www.census.gov/newsroom/press-releases/2018/estimates-national-state.html.

4. Esther Eke, "2017 Idaho Labor Market and Economic Report," Idaho Department of Labor, March 2018, 5, https://www.labor.idaho.gov/dnn/Portals/0/Publications/Labor%20Market%20Report%202017%20-%20FINAL.pdf.

5. Samantha Sharf, "America's Fastest-Growing Cities 2018," *Forbes*, February 28, 2018, https://www.forbes.com/sites/samanthasharf/2018/02/28/americas-fastest-growing-cities-2018/#66bef87445dc.

6. Del Gray, "Rent Squeeze," *Emmett Messenger-Index*, July 17, 2019, https://www.idahopress.com/emmett/news/rent-squeeze/article_a4e36d04-dc36-579a-aabe-7e4182f05dbe.html.

7. Gray, "Rent Squeeze."

8. Gray.

9. Harrison Berry, "The Great Treasure Valley Tradeoff," *Edible Idaho*, June 28, 2018, https://edibleidaho.ediblecommunities.com/food-thought/great-treasure-valley-tradeoff.

10. Tara Golshan, "Brad Little, the Establishment Pick, Wins the Republican Primary in Idaho's Governor's Race," *Vox*, May 16, 2018, https://www.vox.com/2018/5/16/17356416/idaho-governor-race-results-republican-brad-little.

11. Kimberlee Kruesi, "Little Voluntarily Discloses His Financial Assets," *The Spokesman-Review*, November 20, 2017, https://www.spokesman.com/blogs/boise/2017/nov/20/little-voluntarily-discloses-his-financial-assets/.

12. Kruesi, "Little Voluntarily Discloses His Financial Assets."

13. Rigoberto A. Lopez, Adesoji O. Adelaja, and Margaret S. Andrews, "The Effects of Suburbanization on Agriculture," *American Journal of Agricultural Economics* 70, no. 20 (May 1988): 346–58, https://www.researchgate.net/publication/247568666_The_Effects_of_Suburbanization_on_Agriculture.

14. Nicole Foy, "Idaho's Hispanic Population, Economic Impact Continues to grow," *Idaho Statesman*, January 4, 2019, https://www.idahopress.com/news/local/idaho-s-hispanic-population-economic-impact-continues-to-grow/article_0631d850-5896-5752-a703-b7ac183fba0d.html.

15. Foy, "Idaho's Hispanic Population, Economic Impact Continues to Grow."

16. Jeanne Croteau, "Booming Boise: My Relocation to the Fastest Growing City in America," *Forbes*, June 13, 2018, https://www.forbes.com/sites/jeannecroteau/2018/06/13/booming-boise-my-relocation-to-the-fastest-growing-city-in-america/#5aab9da740bd.

17. Morgan Boydston, "Do Californians Feel Welcomed in Idaho?" KTVB.com, May 22, 2018, https://www.ktvb.com/article/news/local/do-californians-feel -welcomed-in-idaho/277-557258526.

18. Joe Parris, "Are Most New Idahoans Really from California?" KTVB.com, November 7, 2019, https://www.ktvb.com/article/news/local/growing-idaho /moving-idaho-california-where-people-going-where-from/277-0865fe64-f289 -4505-8ee5-6ec0292a609c.

19. Adam McCann, "Most and Least Diverse States in America," WalletHub, September 9, 2020, https://wallethub.com/edu/most-least-diverse-states-in-america /38262/#detailed.

20. Daniel C. Vock, "Twin Falls: The Idaho City at the Center of the Refugee Controversy," *Governing*, June 2017, https://www.governing.com/topics/politics /gov-refugees-twin-falls-idaho-immigration.html.

21. Susan Ferriss, "How Trump's Immigration Crackdown Threatens to Choke Idaho's Dairy Industry," *Politico*, September 16, 2017, https://www.politico.com /magazine/story/2017/09/16/trump-immigration-crackdown-idaho-dairy -industry-215608.

22. Kirk Johnson, "What the Fastest Growth in the U.S. Means for Idaho Politics," *The New York Times*, May 13, 2018, https://www.nytimes.com/2018/05/13/us /boise-idaho-primary-election-growth.html.

23. Maria L. La Ganga, "'Go Back to California': Wave of Newcomers Fuels Backlash in Boise," *Los Angeles Times*, November 10, 2019, https://www.latimes.com /california/story/2019-11-10/go-back-to-california-wave-of-newcomers-fuels -backlash-in-boise.

24. Dan Meyer, "Harnessing the Wind of Development," *Edible Idaho*, June 28, 2018, http://edibleidaho.ediblecommunities.com/food-thought/harnessing-wind -development.

25. "Sprawl Costs," New Urbanism, accessed August 15, 2020, http://www.new urbanism.org/sprawlcosts.html.

26. Charles Marohn, "Sprawl Is Not the Problem," Strong Towns, April 18, 2016, https://www.strongtowns.org/journal/2016/4/17/sprawl-is-not-the-problem? rq=suburban%20sprawl.

27. Marohn, "Sprawl Is Not the Problem."

28. Wolf, "Development Takes a Bite Out of Farmland."

29. Rachel Quednau, "Why Walkable Streets Are More Economically Productive," Strong Towns, January 18, 2018, https://www.strongtowns.org/journal /2018/1/16/why-walkable-streets-are-more-economically-productive.

30. Andrew Price, "What Does Incrementalism Actually Mean?" Strong Towns, September 6, 2018, https://www.strongtowns.org/journal/2018/9/5/incre mentalism?rq=incremental.

31. Jenna Narducci, Christian Sprague, Jodi Brandt, Jen Schneider, Jillian Moroney, Michail Fragkias, and Shawn Benner, "Projecting Urban Expansion in the

Treasure Valley to 2100," Boise State University, October 2017, https://www
.boisestate.edu/hes/files/2019/03/Whitepaper-Projecting-Urban-Expansion
-in-the-Treasure-Valley-to-2100.pdf.

32. "Income Tax Incentives for Land Conservation," Land Trust Alliance, accessed August 15, 2020, https://www.landtrustalliance.org/topics/taxes/income-tax -incentives-land-conservation.

33. "Planning Implementation Tools Transfer of Development Rights (TDR)," Center for Land Use Education, November 2005, https://www.uwsp.edu/cnr-ap /clue/Documents/PlanImplementation/Transfer_of_Development_Rights.pdf.

34. Joan Didion, "Notes from a Native Daughter," in *Slouching Towards Bethlehem* (New York: Farrar, Straus and Giroux, 2008), 184.

35. Wolf, "Development Takes a Bite Out of Farmland."

CHAPTER 10

1. John Opie, *The Law of the Land: Two Hundred Years of American Farmland Policy* (Lincoln: University of Nebraska Press, 1994), xxvi.

2. Robert Nisbet, *Quest for Community: A Study in the Ethics of Order and Freedom* (Wilmington, DE: ISI Books, 2010), 2.

3. Alexis de Tocqueville, *Democracy in America* (Chicago: University of Chicago Press, 2000), 487.

4. Tocqueville, *Democracy in America*, 484.

5. Nisbet, *Quest for Community*, 131.

6. Sarah Taber, "America Loves the Idea of Family Farms. That's Unfortunate," *New York*, June 16, 2019, http://nymag.com/intelligencer/2019/06/america-loves -the-idea-of-family-farms-thats-unfortunate.html.

7. Jesse Newman and Patrick McGroarty, "The Next American Farm Bust Is upon Us," *The Wall Street Journal*, February 8, 2017, https://www.wsj.com/articles /the-next-american-farm-bust-is-upon-us-1486572488.

8. Mario Parker, "'The Superpower of Food' Needs Global Trade, U.S. Ag Secretary Says," *Bloomberg*, June 5, 2019, https://www.bloomberg.com/news /articles/2019-06-05/-the-superpower-of-food-needs-global-trade-trump-s -farm-chief. *See also*: Alana Semuels, "'They're Trying to Wipe Us off the Map.' Small American Farmers Are Nearing Extinction," *Time*, November 27, 2019, https://time.com/5736789/small-american-farmers-debt-crisis-extinction/.

9. "New National Poll Shows Impacts of Rural Economy on Farmer Mental Health," American Farm Bureau Federation, May 1, 2019, https://www .fb.org/newsroom/new-national-poll-shows-impacts-of-rural-economy-on -farmer-mental-health.

10. Vann R. Newkirk II, "The Great Land Robbery," *The Atlantic*, September 2019, https://www.theatlantic.com/magazine/archive/2019/09/this-land-was -our-land/594742/.

11. "Commodity Subsidies in the United States Totaled $223.5 Billion from 1995–2019," Environmental Working Group, August 14, 2020, https://farm.ewg.org/progdetail.php?fps=00000&progcode=totalfarm&page=conc&regionname=theUnitedStates.
12. Patrick J. Deneen, *Why Liberalism Failed* (New Haven, CT: Yale University Press, 2018), 194–98.
13. Wendell Berry, *Sex, Economy, Freedom, and Community* (New York: Pantheon Books, 1993), 155.
14. Wendell Berry, *Remembering* (Berkeley, CA: Counterpoint Press, 2008), 38.
15. Berry, *Remembering*, 50.

CHAPTER 11

1. Richard Manning, "Idaho's Sewer System Is the Snake River," *High Country News*, August 11, 2014, https://www.hcn.org/issues/46.13/idahos-sewer-system-is-the-snake-river/@@gallery_view?b_start:int=1#body.
2. Simone Weil, *The Need for Roots: Prelude to a Declaration of Duties towards Mankind* (New York: Routledge Classics, 2002), 45.
3. Timothy Kleiser, "The Pain of Losing One's 'Place,'" *The American Conservative*, June 13, 2020, https://www.theamericanconservative.com/urbs/the-pain-of-losing-ones-place/.
4. Wallace Stegner, *Where the Bluebird Sings to the Lemonade Springs: Living and Writing in the West* (New York: Random House, 2002), xxvii.
5. Robert Nisbet, *Quest for Community: A Study in the Ethics of Order and Freedom* (Wilmington, DE: ISI Books, 2010), 12.
6. Weil, *The Need for Roots*, 43.
7. Edmund Burke, *Reflections on the Revolution in France and Other Writings* (Chicago: Everyman's Library, 2015), 700.

CONCLUSION

1. Robert Nisbet, *Quest for Community: A Study in the Ethics of Order and Freedom* (Wilmington, DE: ISI Books, 2010), 88.
2. Christine Emba, "Liberalism Is Loneliness," *The Washington Post*, April 6, 2018, https://www.washingtonpost.com/opinions/liberalism-is-loneliness/2018/04/06/02a01aec-39ce-11e8-8fd2-49fe3c675a89_story.html.
3. Bruce Katz and Jeremy Nowak, *The New Localism: How Cities Can Thrive in the Age of Populism* (Washington, DC: Brookings Institution, 2017).
4. James Rebanks, *The Shepherd's Life: Modern Dispatches from an Ancient Landscape* (New York: Flatiron Books, 2015), 19.

Index